200 *Fast*
food for friends

hamlyn | all colour cookbook

200 *Fast*
food for friends

An Hachette UK Company

www.hachette.co.uk

First published in Great Britain in 2015 by Hamlyn
a division of Octopus Publishing Group Ltd, Endeavour
House, 189 Shaftesbury Avenue, London, WC2H 8JY
www.octopusbooks.co.uk

ISBN 13: 978-0-600-62902-3

A CIP catalogue record for this book is available
from the British Library.

Printed and bound in China

1 2 3 4 5 6 7 8 9 10

Both metric and imperial measurements have been given
in all recipes. Use one set of measurements only, and not a
mixture of both.

Standard level spoon measurements are used in all recipes.
1 tablespoon = 15 ml spoon
1 teaspoon = 5 ml spoon

Ovens should be preheated to the specified temperature
– if using a fan-assisted oven, follow the manufacturer's
instructions for adjusting the time and temperature.

Fresh herbs should be used unless otherwise stated.

Eggs should be medium unless otherwise stated. The
Department of Health advises that eggs should not be
consumed raw. This book contains dishes made with raw
or lightly cooked eggs. It is prudent for more vulnerable
people such as pregnant and nursing mothers, invalids, the
elderly, babies and young children to avoid uncooked or
lightly cooked dishes made with eggs. Once prepared these
dishes should be kept refrigerated and used promptly.

This book includes dishes made with nuts and nut
derivatives. It is advisable for customers with known allergic
reactions to nuts and nut derivatives and those who may be
potentially vulnerable to these allergies, such as pregnant
and nursing mothers, invalids, the elderly, babies and
children, to avoid dishes made with nuts and nut oils. It is
also prudent to check the labels of pre-prepared ingredients
for the possible inclusion of nut derivatives.

contents

introduction 6

starters & light bites 10

meat & poultry 52

fish & seafood 102

vegetarian 150

desserts 192

index 234

acknowledgements 240

introduction

This book offers a new and flexible approach to meal planning for busy cooks and lets you choose the recipe option that best fits the time you have available. Here you will find over 200 dishes that will inspire and motivate you to get cooking every day of the year.

All the recipes take a maximum of 30 minutes to cook. Some take as little as 20 minutes and, amazingly, many take only 10 minutes.

On every page you'll find a main recipe plus a short-cut version or a fancier variation if you have a bit more time to spare. Whatever you go for, you'll find a huge range of super-quick recipes to get you through the week.

food for friends

Inviting friends and family over for a bite to eat should be the easiest, most enjoyable thing in the world, but too often most of your time is spent slaving in the kitchen rather than having fun and enjoying dinner together. But it's easy to produce delicious, inspiring dishes in less than 30 minutes, and some are so simple they can be on the table in just 10 minutes. Which lets you get on with the important things in life.

get ahead

A bit of planning ahead is always useful when having friends over. Try to think of your guests'

tastes – find out if you need to cater for any special diets or if there is something people especially love to eat – and then decide on your main course. Once you've worked this out, it's easier to decide what else to serve.

Think about timings when planning what you eat. For a larger meal, it's useful to actually write down a time plan of when things need to be started. But no matter the scale of your event, it's always best to cook a few delicious dishes rather than stress out trying to organize an array of mediocre ones. It's a good idea to focus your effort on one dish, so if you choose a complicated starter, keep the main course simple with something like pasta. If you opt for a show-off pudding and main course, make the starter a no-cook salad. When planning your menu, ensure that you think about the washing up. You don't want to be cleaning up the kitchen for hours after your guests have left, so wash up as you go along. If time is really short, cook a one-pot dish; a smart pan that can be taken straight from the hob to the table is a great investment and makes for a relaxing meal.

stress-free cooking

starters

A sit-down starter sets the scene for a formal evening – perhaps a birthday dinner or when you want to impress the parents-in-law – and this book includes a tempting range of simple starter recipes. On other occasions, it is perfectly acceptable to abandon formal starters and set out a selection of nuts, olives and good-quality crisps, served with a cocktail or glass of bubbly. You could provide more substantial nibbles to which guests can help themselves, such as hams and salami, sunblush tomatoes and so on.

main courses

There are plenty of ways of keeping the main course simple and quick. A leg or shoulder of lamb will take quite a while to cook in the oven, but a rack of lamb can be on the table in less than 30 minutes. This makes life easy, but remember that with these leaner, quick-

cooking cuts of meat, it really is worthwhile spending a bit extra to get the best quality – you will taste the difference. Fish and seafood are perfect for the host in a hurry, as they take so little time to cook and need not much more than a squeeze of lemon juice and simple side dish to turn them into a delicious dinner-party treat. Just remember to shop for them on the day you are planning to cook them because fresh fish really does taste better.

Vegetarians can sometimes feel a bit cheated at dinner parties, so to make a meal really special, look out for seasonal ingredients – the first asparagus of the season or a perfectly ripe bunch of tomatoes would be great starting points for a meat-free meal. More unusual heritage vegetables or baby vegetables, which are now widely available, are also a wonderful way of perking up a plate and making it look worthy of a restaurant.

The flavour of good-quality basic ingredients will always shine through, and all it takes to enhance them is a little fresh pesto, a drizzle of special oil or vinegar or a scattering of herbs. Keep side dishes simple and fast – a selection of leaves dressed with something special, or maybe some couscous or polenta, which can be ready in 5 minutes flat. Make the most of canned beans, which can be easily whizzed up to make a quick mash or you can toss them with some dressing and tomatoes to create a hearty salad.

Another way to make the meal a little more special is to use an unusual ingredient. Supermarkets are increasingly catering for our more exotic tastes and an exciting ingredient can elevate a meal to something truly memorable. Look out for jewel-like pomegranate seeds, which look so pretty on the plate and are great to scatter over salads or Middle Eastern dishes. For an Asian dish, try to get some authentic ingredients like lime leaves and lemon grass, which will lend your dish a beautifully subtle and distinctive flavour, or go to the trouble of tracking down a quality curry paste. If you're making a simple Italian supper, search out a different type of pasta than you usually use – perhaps try thick tube-like bucatini or use black squid-ink pasta for a seafood dish. Sometimes it is worth spending a little extra on a key ingredient that can be used sparingly. Creamy rich buffalo mozzarella is a world apart from the regular cows' milk version, while just a hint of perfumed saffron will transform a paella. It's also worth remembering that a splash of alcohol really helps to lift a dish – brandy or wine for a classic French dish, a drop of vermouth for fish or try sherry for a Spanish feel.

pudding
To round off the meal in style you'll want to prepare something delectable, but this doesn't have to be complicated. Browse through the pudding recipes for inspiration, choosing a 10-minute recipe if you are short on time. For a really stress-free evening, serve a selection of great cheeses with some walnuts and perhaps a bottle of sweet wine, or a colourful bowl of exotic fruit salad.

what to do if it all goes wrong
Even the best, most experienced cook will have nights when things go wrong in the kitchen. The most important thing is not to panic: a relaxed, welcoming host is what makes the evening. And the chances are that no one will notice anyway – a name change is often all that is needed.

starters & light bites

bloody mary gazpacho

Serves **4**
Total cooking time **10 minutes**

2 **garlic cloves**, chopped
2 **celery sticks**, chopped, plus
    extra, preferably with leaves,
    to serve
1 tablespoon chopped **onion**
500 g (1 lb) **ripe tomatoes**
300 ml (½ pint) **tomato juice**
juice of 2 **limes**
1 teaspoon **celery salt**
2–3 tablespoons
    Worcestershire sauce
125 ml (4 fl oz) **vodka**
    (optional)
Tabasco sauce, to taste

To serve
lime wedges
ice cubes

Put all the ingredients, except the vodka and Tabasco sauce, in a food processor or blender and whizz until smooth. Press the mixture through a fine sieve to remove all the tomato pulp.

Add the vodka, if using, and Tabasco sauce to taste, then pour into glasses with some ice cubes. Serve with celery sticks and lime wedges for squeezing over.

For roasted tomato gazpacho, toss 500 g (1 lb) halved tomatoes with 3 tablespoons olive oil. Place in a roasting tin with 2 peeled garlic cloves and cook in a preheated oven, 200°C (400°F), Gas Mark 6, for 20 minutes or until soft and lightly browned. Place in a food processor or blender with 1 drained ready-roasted red pepper from a jar, 2 teaspoons sherry vinegar, 1 crustless slice of bread and 300 ml (½ pint) tomato juice and whizz until smooth. Rub through a fine sieve to remove all the tomato pulp, then season and add a little Tabasco sauce to taste. Chill in the freezer for 5 minutes, then ladle into serving bowls. Scatter over 1 tablespoon chopped red onion mixed together with 1 stoned, peeled and diced avocado. **Total cooking time 30 minutes.**

corn cakes with smoked salmon

Serves **4**
Total cooking time **20 minutes**

2 **eggs**, beaten
4 tablespoons **milk**
300 g (10 oz) canned
   sweetcorn kernels, drained
75 g (3 oz) **self-raising flour**
2 **spring onions**, sliced
2 tablespoons **vegetable oil**
150 g (5 oz) **smoked salmon**
4 tablespoons **mascarpone**
   cheese
salt and **pepper**
chopped **chives**, to garnish

Beat together the eggs, milk, sweetcorn, flour and spring onions in a bowl until you have a smooth batter. Season well.

Heat 1 tablespoon of the oil in a large, nonstick frying pan. Add half the batter to the pan in separate spoonfuls to make 6 small pancakes. Cook for 2–3 minutes on each side until golden and cooked through. Set aside on kitchen paper while you cook the remaining batter.

Pile the pancakes on to serving plates and arrange the smoked salmon and mascarpone on top. Scatter with the chives and serve.

For corn & salmon pasta, cook 400 g (13 oz) fresh penne according to the packet instructions until al dente. Add 125 g (4 oz) frozen sweetcorn kernels for the last 1 minute of cooking. Drain and return to the pan. Stir in 5 tablespoons crème fraîche and 150 g (5 oz) smoked salmon, torn into strips. Scatter over a handful of chives, chopped, to serve. **Total cooking time 10 minutes.**

hot potato blinis with beetroot

Serves **4**

Total cooking time **30 minutes**

200 g (7 oz) **ready-made mashed potato**
50 g (2 oz) **self-raising flour**
3 large **eggs**, separated
2 tablespoons **soured cream**
4 tablespoons finely chopped **dill**
vegetable oil, for frying
salt and **pepper**

For the topping
2 **cooked beetroot**, peeled and finely diced
6 tablespoons **crème fraîche**
1 tablespoon **creamed horseradish**
salt and **pepper**
chopped **chives**, to garnish

Place the mashed potato in a bowl. Beat in the flour, egg yolks, soured cream and dill and season well.

Whisk the egg whites in a large, grease-free bowl until stiff. Using a metal spoon, carefully fold the beaten egg whites into the potato mixture.

Heat a little oil in a large, nonstick frying pan. Add 3–4 separate tablespoons of the potato blini mixture. Fry over a medium heat until set, then turn the potato blinis over and fry briefly so that both sides are lightly browned. Remove and keep warm in a low oven. Repeat the process until all the potato mixture has been used.

Meanwhile, mix together most of the beetroot, reserving a little to garnish, crème fraîche and creamed horseradish and season well.

Spoon the beetroot mixture over the blinis, garnish with the reserved beetroot, chopped chives and freshly ground black pepper.

For potato & chive soup, melt 25 g (1 oz) butter in a saucepan. When it begins to foam, add 1 diced onion and toss in the butter until well coated. Stir in 425 g (14 oz) ready-made mashed potato and 900 ml (1½ pints) hot vegetable stock. Bring to the boil and add 125 ml (4 fl oz) milk. Purée the soup with a hand-held blender. Season to taste. Stir in 3 tablespoons each very finely chopped dill and chives. Serve immediately with crusty bread. **Total cooking time 20 minutes.**

crayfish cocktail

Serves **4**
Total cooking time **10 minutes**

5 tablespoons **mayonnaise**
2 tablespoons **tomato ketchup**
Tabasco sauce, to taste
lemon juice, to taste
300 g (10 oz) **cooked peeled crayfish tails**
2 **Little Gem lettuces**, leaves separated
2 small **ripe avocado**, stoned, peeled and sliced
salt and **pepper**
paprika, to garnish

Mix together the mayonnaise and ketchup in a bowl, add Tabasco sauce and lemon juice to taste and season. Stir through the crayfish.

Arrange the lettuce leaves in serving dishes with the avocado slices. Spoon over the crayfish mixture. Sprinkle with some paprika to garnish.

For Mexican-style seafood cocktail, place 150 g (5 oz) raw peeled prawns in a bowl. Pour over boiling water to cover and leave for 2 minutes. Add 150 g (5 oz) shelled and cleaned scallops, adding a little more boiling water, and leave for a further 3 minutes, then drain. Mix together 300 ml (½ pint) tomato juice, 1 tablespoon tomato ketchup, a good squeeze of lime juice and Tabasco sauce to taste. Stir together with the seafood and leave to stand for 10 minutes. Spoon into serving bowls. Top with 1 stoned, peeled and chopped avocado, 1 sliced spring onion and a handful of chopped fresh coriander. **Total cooking time 20 minutes.**

baked figs wrapped in prosciutto

Serves **4**
Total cooking time **20 minutes**

8 **figs**
125 g (4 oz) **mozzarella
  cheese**, cut into 8 slices
8 slices of **prosciutto**
7 tablespoons **olive oil**
2 tablespoons **balsamic
  vinegar**
125 g (4 oz) **rocket leaves**
salt and **pepper**

Cut a deep cross into the top of each fig, nearly to the bottom, then place a slice of mozzarella inside. Wrap a slice of prosciutto around each fig. Brush the prosciutto with a little of the oil. Transfer to a baking sheet and cook in a preheated oven, 220°C (425°F), Gas Mark 7, for 7–10 minutes or until the ham is crisp and the cheese starts to melt.

Meanwhile, whisk the balsamic vinegar with the remaining oil and season well.

Toss most of the dressing with the rocket leaves and arrange on plates. Add the baked figs and drizzle with a little more of the dressing. Serve immediately.

For fig & ham country salad, halve 8 figs and brush them with a little olive oil. Heat a griddle pan until smoking and then cook the cut sides of the figs for 1 minute until lightly charred. Wrap each half in a slice of prosciutto. Mix 1 tablespoon finely chopped shallot with 1 tablespoon sherry vinegar and 3 tablespoons olive oil. Toss through 150 g (5 oz) salad leaves and serve with the griddled figs with some soft goats' cheese crumbled on top. **Total cooking time 10 minutes.**

vietnamese spring rolls

Serves **4**
Total cooking time **30 minutes**

vegetable oil, for frying
125 g (4 oz) **lean minced pork**
100 g (3½ oz) small **raw peeled prawns**
50 g (2 oz) **cooked crabmeat**
1 **garlic clove**, crushed
1 teaspoon finely chopped **fresh root ginger**
2 **spring onions**, finely chopped
1 tablespoon **soy sauce**
pinch of **caster sugar**
handful of **fresh coriander**, chopped
50 g (2 oz) **dried fine rice noodles**
1 tablespoon **cornflour**
1 tablespoon **water**
12 **spring roll wrappers**
salt and **pepper**

To serve
chilli sauce
herb salad (optional)

Heat 1 tablespoon oil in a wok or large frying pan. Add the pork, prawns, crabmeat, garlic, ginger and spring onions and stir-fry for 5 minutes until just cooked through. Stir in the soy sauce and sugar and heat until bubbling, then stir in the coriander and set aside to cool a little.

Meanwhile, prepare the noodles according to the instructions on the packet, then drain and add to the seafood mixture.

Mix the cornflour with the measurement water. Place a tablespoon of the seafood mixture on 1 spring roll wrapper. Brush the side with a little of the cornflour mixture, then fold over and roll up. Repeat with the remaining seafood mixture and wrappers.

Fill a large, deep saucepan one-third full of oil and heat until a cube of bread browns in 15 seconds. Deep-fry the rolls in batches for 3 minutes until golden and crisp, keeping the cooked rolls warm in a low oven. Drain on kitchen paper. Serve with chilli sauce for dipping and a herb salad, if liked.

For Vietnamese summer rolls, prepare 50 g (2 oz) dried fine rice noodles according to the instructions on the packet. Drain. Soften 12 rice paper wrappers in very hot water for 30 seconds. Place on damp kitchen paper. Add some noodles, 2 cooked peeled prawns, some chopped lettuce, cored, deseeded and sliced red pepper, sliced carrot and chopped fresh coriander to each wrapper. Moisten the edges, fold over and roll up. Serve with chilli sauce for dipping. **Total cooking time 20 minutes.**

baked mushrooms with taleggio

Serves **4**

Total cooking time **20 minutes**

8 large **flat mushrooms,** trimmed

8 slices of **Taleggio cheese**

75 g (3 oz) **dried breadcrumbs**

1 **garlic clove,** crushed

6 tablespoons **olive oil**

bunch of **basil leaves,** finely chopped

25 g (1 oz) **Parmesan cheese,** finely grated

25 g (1 oz) **pine nuts,** toasted and chopped, plus extra to serve

salt and **pepper**

Put the mushrooms, cap-side down, on a baking sheet and top each one with a slice of Taleggio. Mix together the breadcrumbs and garlic and scatter a little over each mushroom. Drizzle with some of the olive oil and bake in a preheated oven, 200°C (400°F), Gas Mark 6, for 15–20 minutes until golden and crispy.

Meanwhile, mix together the basil, Parmesan cheese, pine nuts and remaining oil and season to taste.

Drizzle the pesto over the baked mushrooms and scatter over a few extra pine nuts to serve.

For leek & mushroom bake, heat 2 tablespoons oil in a frying pan, add 1 cleaned, trimmed and thinly sliced leek and 125 g (4 oz) trimmed and sliced mushrooms and cook for 3–5 minutes until softened. Meanwhile, whisk 6 eggs with 50 ml (2 fl oz) double cream and a handful of chopped basil. Stir in the softened vegetables. Season to taste and pour the mixture into a greased 20 cm (8 inch) square cake tin. Scatter over 25 g (1 oz) grated Parmesan cheese and bake in a preheated oven, 180°C (350°F), Gas Mark 4, for 25 minutes until just set. **Total cooking time 30 minutes.**

celeriac remoulade with ham

Serves **6**

Total cooking time **10 minutes**

5 tablespoons **mayonnaise**
1 tablespoon **Dijon mustard**
2 tablespoons **crème fraîche**
1 small **celeriac**, peeled and
  cut into fine matchsticks
handful of **parsley**, finely
  chopped
6 slices of **Bayonne** or **Parma
  ham**
salt and **pepper**

Mix together the mayonnaise, mustard and crème fraîche in a bowl until smooth. Season to taste, add the celeriac and parsley and stir together.

Spoon the mixture on to serving plates along with the slices of ham.

For celeriac remoulade & ham rolls, whisk together 2 egg yolks and 1 teaspoon Dijon mustard, then slowly whisk in 300 ml (½ pint) olive oil, at first one drop at a time and then in a slow, steady stream, until creamy. Season to taste with lemon juice and salt and pepper. Stir through 1 tablespoon drained capers and a handful each of chopped parsley and chives. Peel ½ celeriac and cut into thin matchsticks, then stir together with the mayonnaise. Spoon a little of the celeriac on to one end of a slice of ham and roll up, repeating to make 12 rolls. Arrange them on a plate with sprigs of watercress. **Total cooking time 20 minutes.**

tomato, prawn & feta salad

Serves **4**

Total cooking time **30 minutes**

200 g (7 oz) **cherry tomatoes,** halved

5 tablespoons **olive oil,** plus extra for oiling

handful of **oregano leaves,** chopped

1 teaspoon crushed **fennel seeds**

1 tablespoon **balsamic vinegar**

150 g (5 oz) large **cooked peeled prawns,** tails on

100 g (3½ oz) **rocket leaves**

75 g (3 oz) **feta cheese,** crumbled

salt and **pepper**

Place the tomatoes, cut-side up, on a lightly oiled baking sheet. Drizzle over the oil, season with salt and pepper, then sprinkle a little of the oregano and crushed fennel seeds over each tomato. Place in a preheated oven, 200˚C (400˚F), Gas Mark 6, and cook for 15–20 minutes until browned and slightly shrivelled. Leave to cool for a few minutes.

Toss the juices from the baking sheet with the balsamic vinegar and prawns. Then arrange on a serving plate with the rocket and cooked tomatoes. Scatter over the feta and serve.

For prawns with sundried tomato feta dip, mash together 75 g (3 oz) cream cheese and 25 g (1 oz) feta cheese until smooth, then thin with a little milk. Stir in 3 drained and chopped sundried tomatoes in oil and a handful of basil, chopped. Arrange 200 g (7 oz) cooked large peeled prawns on a serving plate and serve with the dip. **Total cooking time 10 minutes.**

asparagus mimosa

Serves **4**
Total cooking time **20 minutes**

6 **quails' or** 2 **hens' eggs**
200 g (7 oz) **asparagus
spears**, trimmed
1 teaspoon **Dijon mustard**
1 tablespoon **white wine
vinegar**
1 tablespoon **single cream**
75 ml (3 fl oz) **olive oil**
1 tablespoon drained **capers**
50 g (2 oz) **pitted black
olives**, chopped
salt and **pepper**

Bring a saucepan of water to the boil and gently lower in the eggs. Cook the quails' eggs for 5 minutes or the hens' eggs for 8 minutes. Remove from the pan and cool under cold running water.

Meanwhile, cook the asparagus in a pan of lightly salted boiling water for 3–5 minutes until just tender, drain and cool under cold running water.

Stir together the mustard, vinegar and cream and then slowly whisk in the oil, a little at a time. Season well.

Arrange the asparagus on 4 plates and drizzle over the dressing. Shell and roughly chop the eggs, then scatter over the asparagus together with the capers and olives.

For asparagus tart, mix together 2 beaten eggs with 150 g (5 oz) mascarpone cheese and 50 g (2 oz) grated Parmesan cheese. Place a 375 g (12 oz) sheet of ready-rolled puff pastry on a lightly greased baking sheet. Score a 1 cm (½ inch) border around the pastry. Spread the egg mixture all over the pastry inside the border, then arrange 200 g (7 oz) asparagus spears, trimmed, on top together with 25 g (1 oz) roughly chopped pitted black olives. Drizzle over 1 tablespoon olive oil and bake in a preheated oven, 200°C (400°F), Gas Mark 6, for 15–20 minutes until golden and puffed. **Total cooking time 30 minutes.**

tarragon mushroom toasts

Serves **4**
Total cooking time **20 minutes**

8 slices of **brioche**
150 g (5 oz) **butter**
2 **banana shallots**, finely
  chopped
3 **garlic cloves**, finely chopped
1 **red chilli**, deseeded and
  finely chopped (optional)
300 g (10 oz) **mixed wild
  mushrooms**, such as
  chanterelle, cep, girolle and
  oyster, trimmed and sliced
4 tablespoons **crème fraîche**,
  plus extra to garnish
  (optional)
2 tablespoons finely chopped
  tarragon
1 tablespoon finely chopped
  flat leaf parsley
salt and **pepper**

Toast the brioche slices lightly and keep warm.

Heat the butter in a frying pan and sauté the shallots, garlic and chilli, if using, for 1–2 minutes. Add the mushrooms and stir-fry over a medium heat for 6–8 minutes. Season well, remove from the heat and stir in the crème fraîche and chopped herbs.

Spoon the mushrooms on to the toasted brioche and serve immediately, with an extra dollop of crème fraîche, if liked.

For chunky mushroom & tarragon soup, heat 2 x 400 g (13 oz) cans cream of mushroom soup in a saucepan along with 2 x 300 g (10 oz) cans whole button mushrooms. Bring to the boil, then reduce the heat and simmer for 2–3 minutes until piping hot. Stir in 25 g (1 oz) chopped tarragon and serve immediately, garnished with a little chopped flat leaf parsley. **Total cooking time 10 minutes.**

salt & pepper squid bites

Serves **4–6**
Total cooking time **20 minutes**

500 g (1 lb) **cleaned squid**
2 teaspoons **black peppercorns**, crushed
1 teaspoon **chilli flakes**
2 teaspoons **salt**
100 g (3½ oz) **plain flour**
vegetable oil, for deep-frying
2 **spring onions**, cut into thick slices
1 **red chilli**, cut into thick strips
lemon wedges, to serve

Cut each squid tube in half. Lay flat, inside up, and use a sharp knife to gently score across. Cut into bite-sized pieces, then pat dry with kitchen paper.

Mix together the crushed peppercorns, chilli flakes, salt and flour in a bowl. Toss the squid in the mixture.

Fill a large, deep saucepan one-third full with oil and heat until a cube of bread browns in 15 seconds. Shake off the excess flour from a handful of squid and deep-fry for 2–3 minutes until just golden and crisp. Drain on kitchen paper. Keep warm in a low oven. Repeat with the remaining squid.

Deep-fry the spring onions and chilli strips for 1–2 minutes, and use to garnish the squid. Serve with lemon wedges for squeezing over.

For salt & pepper squid bites with chilli jam, for the chilli jam, place 2 large tomatoes in a saucepan with 200 g (7 oz) caster sugar and 4 finely chopped red chillies. Add 50 ml (2 fl oz) cider vinegar, 1 tablespoon fish sauce and a squeeze of lime juice. Bring to the boil and let the mixture bubble until the sugar melts. Then simmer for 20 minutes until sticky and thickened. Meanwhile, prepare and deep-fry the squid as above. Serve the squid hot with the chilli jam. **Total cooking time 30 minutes.**

crab & mango salad

Serves **4**

Total cooking time **20 minutes**

50 g (2 oz) **caster sugar**
75 ml (3 fl oz) **water**
2 tablespoons **mirin**
1 **red chilli**, sliced
1 **kaffir lime leaf**, shredded
finely grated rind and juice of
   1 **lime**
1 **mango**, peeled, stoned and
   chopped
75 g (3 oz) **radishes**, halved
½ **cucumber**, sliced
125 g (4 oz) **watercress**
200 g (7 oz) **cooked fresh
   crabmeat**

Put the sugar, measurement water and mirin in a small saucepan, bring to the boil and cook for 3 minutes until it starts to turn syrupy. Stir in the chilli, lime leaf and lime rind and add lime juice to taste. Set aside for 5 minutes.

Toss together the mango, radishes, cucumber and watercress and arrange on serving plates. Sprinkle the crabmeat on top and then drizzle over the dressing.

For wild rice, crab & mango salad, bring a large saucepan of lightly salted water to the boil, add 200 g (7 oz) mixed wild and basmati rice and cook for 25 minutes or according to the instructions on the packet until just tender. Drain and rinse under cold running water to cool. Meanwhile, mix 1 tablespoon finely chopped red onion with 1 teaspoon finely chopped fresh root ginger, 1 finely chopped red chilli, the finely grated rind and juice of 1 lime and 3 tablespoons olive oil. Add the rice, a large handful of chopped fresh coriander, 1 peeled, stoned and chopped mango and 150 g (5 oz) cooked fresh crabmeat, stir well and serve. **Total cooking time 30 minutes.**

moules marinières

Serves **4**
Total cooking time **15 minutes**

2 tablespoons **olive oil**
2 **garlic cloves**, sliced
1.5 kg (3 lb) **live mussels**,
  scrubbed and debearded
200 ml (7 fl oz) **dry white
  wine**
handful of **flat leaf parsley**,
  chopped
crusty bread, to serve

Heat the oil in a large saucepan. Add the garlic and cook for 30 seconds until lightly golden. Add the mussels, discarding any that are cracked or don't shut when tapped, and the wine.

Cover the pan and cook for 5 minutes, shaking the pan occasionally, or until the mussels have opened. Discard any that remain closed.

Stir in the parsley, then serve with crusty bread.

For crispy baked mussels, heat 2 tablespoons olive oil in a large saucepan. Cook 2 sliced garlic cloves for 30 seconds until lightly golden. Add 1.5 kg (3 lb) live mussels, scrubbed and debearded, discarding any that are cracked or don't shut when tapped, and 200 ml (7 fl oz) dry white wine, then season with salt. Cover and cook for 4 minutes, shaking the pan occasionally, until the mussels are just starting to open. Strain, reserving the liquid. Leave to cool a little, then discard any mussels that remain closed. Discard one half-shell from each mussel, leaving the mussels inside the remaining half-shells. Arrange on a baking sheet. Boil the reserved liquid until reduced to 50 ml (2 fl oz). Stir in 100 ml (3½ fl oz) double cream and boil until reduced to 75 ml (3 fl oz). Stir through a handful of flat leaf parsley, chopped. Spoon a little of the sauce over each mussel in its half-shell. Carefully sprinkle each mussel with some dried breadcrumbs and top with a small knob of butter. Place in a preheated oven, 220°C (425°F), Gas Mark 7, for 5 minutes or until golden and bubbling. **Total cooking time 30 minutes.**

broad bean & anchovy salad

Serves **4**
Total cooking time **20 minutes**

1.25 kg (2½ lb) **fresh** or
  frozen broad beans
3 tablespoons **olive oil**
450 g (14½ oz) **cherry
  tomatoes**, halved
6 **spring onions**, sliced
2 **garlic cloves**, finely sliced
6 **anchovy fillets in oil**,
  drained and chopped
1 tablespoon shredded **basil
  leaves**
1 tablespoon chopped **parsley**
50 g (2 oz) **rocket leaves**
2 tablespoons **Parmesan
  cheese** shavings, to serve

Blanch the broad beans in a saucepan of boiling water
for 1 minute. Drain and refresh under cold running
water. Peel off the outer skins.

Heat the olive oil in a frying pan and cook the tomatoes
over a medium heat for 4–5 minutes.

Add the spring onions and garlic and cook for a further
1–2 minutes, then add the broad beans.

Stir in the anchovies and herbs and cook for another
1–2 minutes.

Spoon into a large serving bowl, toss with the rocket
leaves and serve topped with the Parmesan shavings.

For roasted peppers with tomatoes & anchovies,
place 4 halved, cored and deseeded peppers, cut-
side up, in a roasting tin. Halve 8 tomatoes and divide
between the peppers. Top each one with 1–2 anchovy
fillets, a few slices of garlic and a few rosemary sprigs.
Drizzle with 2–3 tablespoons olive oil, season with
pepper and bake in a preheated oven, 200°C (400°F),
Gas Mark 6, for 22–25 minutes. **Total cooking time
30 minutes.**

blue cheese soufflé

Serves **6**
Total cooking time **30 minutes**

75 g (3 oz) crustless
    sourdough bread, cut into
    chunks
250 ml (8 fl oz) **milk**
150 g (5 oz) **blue cheese,**
    crumbled
50 g (2 oz) **butter,** softened,
    plus extra for greasing
4 **eggs,** separated
1 tablespoon **white wine**
    vinegar
3 tablespoons **olive oil**
1 teaspoon **walnut oil**
1 **red apple,** cored and thinly
    sliced
handful of **rocket leaves**
salt and **pepper**

Put the bread in a bowl and pour over the milk. Leave to soak for 5 minutes, then squeeze any excess milk from the bread. Transfer the bread to a food processor or blender with the cheese, butter and egg yolks and blend until smooth. Season to taste.

Whisk the egg whites in a large, grease-free bowl until stiff peaks form. Stir a large spoonful into the cheese mixture, then carefully fold in the remainder, half at a time.

Spoon the mixture into 6 x 150 ml (¼ pint) well-greased ramekins and bake in a preheated oven, 220°C (425°F), Gas Mark 7, for 10–15 minutes until puffed and golden.

Meanwhile, whisk together the vinegar, olive oil and walnut oil and season to taste. Toss together with the apple and rocket leaves.

Serve the soufflés immediately with the dressed rocket and apple alongside.

For blue cheese Waldorf salad, mash 75 g (3 oz) blue cheese with 6 tablespoons mayonnaise. Stir together with 3 cored and chopped apples, 6 chopped celery sticks, 2 sliced spring onions and 50 g (2 oz) toasted chopped walnuts. Place in a serving dish and scatter over some more walnuts, blue cheese and celery leaves to serve. **Total cooking time 10 minutes.**

pear, walnut & gorgonzola salad

Serves **4**
Total cooking time **10 minutes**

3 tablespoons **extra virgin
olive oil**
1 teaspoon **Dijon mustard**
1 tablespoon **white wine
vinegar**
1 teaspoon **caster sugar**
40 g (1½ oz) **walnut pieces**
1 **radicchio**, leaves separated
50 g (2 oz) **rocket leaves**
1 **Cos lettuce heart**, leaves
separated and torn
2 **pears**, cored and sliced
175 g (6 oz) **Gorgonzola
cheese**, crumbled

Whisk together the olive oil, mustard, vinegar and sugar in a small bowl or measuring jug.

Toast the walnut pieces in a dry frying pan until golden, to help bring out their flavour.

Toss together the radicchio, rocket and Cos heart leaves in a bowl. Divide the leaves between 4 plates and sprinkle with the slices of pear, crumbled Gorgonzola and the walnuts.

Pour over the dressing and serve.

For Gorgonzola with warm Marsala pears, place 4 x 100 g (3½ oz) slices of Gorgonzola cheese in a serving dish. Core and cut 2 pears into eighths. Heat 1 tablespoon olive oil in a frying pan and cook the pears for 3–4 minutes on each side. Whisk together 2 tablespoons each clear honey and Marsala, then pour into the pan, letting it simmer and thicken for a few minutes. Using a slotted spoon, remove the pears and place them on top of the Gorgonzola. Fry 65 g (2½ oz) walnut halves in the remaining syrup in the pan. Pour the syrup and walnuts over the pears and Gorgonzola to serve. **Total cooking time 20 minutes.**

cheese-stuffed onions

Serves **4**
Total cooking time **30 minutes**

4 large **onions**, peeled
1 tablespoon **olive oil**
150 g (5 oz) **spinach leaves**
100 g (3½ oz) **ricotta cheese**
1 **egg yolk**
1 teaspoon chopped **thyme leaves**
25 g (1 oz) **Fontina cheese**
40 g (1½ oz) **Parmesan cheese**, grated
25 g (1 oz) **butter**

To serve
50 g (2 oz) **rocket leaves**
3 tablespoons **balsamic syrup**

Blanch the onions in boiling water for 5 minutes. Drain and leave to cool for 5 minutes.

Meanwhile, heat the oil in a large saucepan, add the spinach and cook until wilted. Remove from the pan and roughly chop. Place in a bowl with the ricotta, egg yolk, thyme, Fontina and 20 g (¾ oz) of the grated Parmesan.

Slice off the top of each onion and remove the middle sections with a fork.

Spoon the cheese mixture into the onions and place them in a roasting tin. Sprinkle over the remaining Parmesan, dot with the butter and roast in a preheated oven, 200°C (400°F), Gas Mark 6, for 15 minutes until the cheese is bubbling and golden.

Serve on a bed of rocket leaves, drizzled with the balsamic syrup.

For cheese & onion bruschetta, heat 1 tablespoon olive oil in a frying pan and sauté 1 large sliced onion for 2–3 minutes until soft. Stir in ½ teaspoon sugar and 1 teaspoon balsamic vinegar and cook for a further 1–2 minutes. Toast 8 slices of ciabatta on both sides. Top each one with the caramelized onions and 100 g (3½ oz) crumbled Gorgonzola cheese. Cook under a preheated hot grill until the cheese is golden and bubbling. **Total cooking time 15 minutes.**

caesar salad

Serves **4**
Total cooking time **20 minutes**

½ **baguette**, torn into chunks
2 tablespoons **olive oil**
12 **quails' eggs**
1 **garlic clove**, crushed
2 **anchovy fillets in oil**,
  drained and very finely
  chopped
2 tablespoons **crème fraîche**
1 teaspoon **Dijon mustard**
4 tablespoons **extra virgin
  olive oil**
25 g (1 oz) **Parmesan
  cheese**, grated, plus extra
  shavings to serve
lemon juice, to taste
2 **baby Cos lettuces**, leaves
  separated
pepper

Toss the baguette chunks with the olive oil, transfer to a baking sheet and bake in a preheated oven, 200°C (400°F), Gas Mark 6, for 7–10 minutes until golden and crisp. Leave to cool.

Meanwhile, bring a saucepan of water to the boil, gently lower the eggs and cook for 5 minutes. Remove from the pan and cool under cold running water. Shell and halve.

Mix together the garlic, anchovies, crème fraîche and mustard in a bowl, then slowly whisk in the extra virgin olive oil. Stir through the grated Parmesan, season with pepper and stir in lemon juice to taste.

Arrange the salad leaves on plates along with the baguette chunks and eggs. Drizzle over the sauce and scatter over Parmesan shavings to serve.

For open chicken caesar sandwich, mash 1 drained anchovy fillet in oil and mix with 4 tablespoons mayonnaise, a handful of grated Parmesan cheese and 1 tablespoon lemon juice. Spread over 4 slices of lightly toasted bread and top with 1 baby Cos lettuce, roughly chopped. Place 2 sliced ready-cooked chicken breasts on top and grate a little more Parmesan over the sandwiches. **Total cooking time 10 minutes.**

brie & thyme melts

Serves **4**

Total cooking time **10 minutes**

1 **ciabatta-style loaf**, cut in
  half horizontally
6 tablespoons **onion** or
  caramelized onion chutney
200 g (7 oz) **Brie** or
  Camembert cheese, sliced
1 teaspoon **dried thyme**
4 teaspoons **chilli, garlic** or
  basil oil
tomato salad, to serve
  (optional)

Cut the 2 pieces of bread in half to give 4 portions.
Arrange, cut-side up, on a baking sheet and spread
each piece with the onion chutney.

Lay the cheese slices on top and sprinkle with the
thyme. Drizzle with the flavoured oil and cook under a
preheated hot grill for 3–4 minutes until the cheese
begins to melt. Serve immediately with a tomato salad,
if liked.

For whole baked cheese with garlic & thyme, cut
some little slits in the top of a whole 250 g (8 oz) round
Camembert or baby Brie. Insert 1 thinly sliced garlic
clove and 5–6 small thyme sprigs into the slits. Drizzle
with 2 teaspoons chilli, garlic or basil oil, then wrap in a
loose foil parcel and bake in a preheated oven, 180°C
(350°F), Gas Mark 4, for about 15 minutes until soft
and oozing. Serve with toasted ciabatta, onion chutney
and a tomato salad. **Total cooking time 20 minutes.**

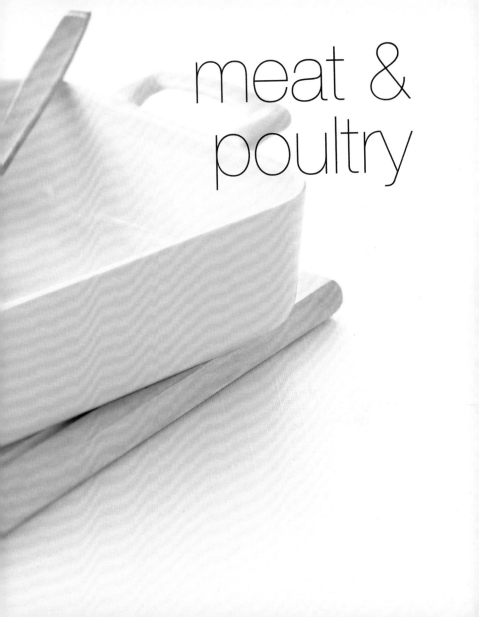

meat & poultry

beef skewers with satay sauce

Serves **4**
Total cooking time **30 minutes**

350 g (11½ oz) **rump** or
  sirloin steak

6 tablespoons **dark soy sauce**

2 tablespoons **sesame oil**

2 tablespoons **rice vinegar**
  or **mirin**

1 tablespoon **soft dark brown**
  sugar

2.5 cm (1 inch) piece of **fresh**
  root ginger, peeled and
  finely grated

1 **garlic clove**, crushed

crudités, such as carrots,
  sugar snap peas and
  cucumber, to serve

For the sauce

6 tablespoons **crunchy**
  peanut butter

3 tablespoons **dark soy sauce**

1 small **red chilli**, finely
  chopped

150 ml (¼ pint) **boiling water**

Cut the steak into long, thin strips. Mix together the soy sauce, oil, vinegar or mirin, sugar, ginger and garlic in a non-metallic bowl. Add the steak and toss well to coat. Cover and leave to marinate for 15 minutes.

Meanwhile, heat all the ingredients for the sauce in a saucepan over a very gentle heat, stirring continuously with a wooden spoon, until smooth and thick. Transfer to a small serving bowl and place on a serving platter with the crudités.

Thread the beef on to 8 metal skewers, or bamboo skewers presoaked in cold water for 30 minutes, and cook under a preheated hot grill for 2 minutes on each side until browned and just cooked.

Transfer to the serving platter with the sauce and crudités and serve immediately.

For Asian-style teriyaki beef on lettuce platters, slice 350 g (11½ oz) trimmed sirloin steak into thin slices and mix with 2 tablespoons bottled teriyaki marinade in a bowl. In a separate bowl, mix ½ cucumber, diced, with 2 tablespoons chopped fresh coriander, 1 teaspoon chilli flakes and the juice of 1 lime. Heat 1 teaspoon vegetable oil in a large frying pan and cook the steak over a high heat for 1 minute on each side. Pile the cucumber mixture into 8 Little Gem lettuce leaves, top with the beef and scatter with chopped spring onions. **Total cooking time 15 minutes.**

beef carpaccio & bean salad

Serves **4**
Total cooking time **30 minutes**

250 g (8 oz) **beef fillet**
3 tablespoons **extra virgin
olive oil**
1 teaspoon **freshly ground
black pepper**
1 tablespoon chopped **thyme
leaves**
1 teaspoon **Dijon mustard**
½ tablespoon **balsamic
vinegar**
½ teaspoon **clear honey**
125 g (4 oz) **green beans**
400 g (13 oz) can **cannellini
beans**, rinsed and drained
1 **red onion**, finely sliced
25g (1 oz) **Parmesan cheese**
shavings, to garnish

Place the beef fillet on a chopping board and rub with
1 tablespoon of the oil, the pepper and the thyme. Wrap
in clingfilm and place in the freezer for 20 minutes.

Meanwhile, whisk together the remaining oil with the
mustard, vinegar and honey to make a dressing.

Blanch the green beans for 2–3 minutes in boiling
water, then drain and refresh under cold running water.
Toss the green beans, cannellini beans and onion in the
dressing and leave to stand at room temperature until
the beef finishes chilling.

Unwrap the beef fillet, slice as thinly as possible and
arrange on a platter. Spoon over the bean salad, with
all the dressing, and garnish with Parmesan shavings.

For quick beef carpaccio & bean salad, whisk
together 3 tablespoons olive oil, 1 tablespoon balsamic
vinegar, 1 teaspoon mustard and 1 teaspoon clear honey.
Blanch 125 g (4 oz) green beans for 2–3 minutes in
boiling water, then drain and refresh under cold running
water. Toss in the dressing with a 400 g (13 oz) can
cannellini beans, rinsed and drained, and leave to
stand at room temperature while preparing the beef.
Arrange 200 g (7 oz) ready-prepared thinly sliced beef
carpaccio on a platter, spoon over the bean salad and
garnish with Parmesan shavings. **Total cooking time
15 minutes.**

hoisin chicken pancakes

Serves **4**

Total cooking time **20 minutes**

1 tablespoon **vegetable oil**

3 **skinless chicken breast fillets**, about 150 g (5 oz) each, cut into strips

2 tablespoons **hoisin sauce**, plus extra for dipping

½ teaspoon **ginger paste**

2 teaspoons **dark soy sauce**

8 **rice flour pancakes** (the sort used for crispy duck)

125 g (4 oz) **bean sprouts**, blanched in boiling water for 30 seconds, drained and refreshed under cold running water

4 **spring onions**, cut into thin strips

½ **cucumber**, cut into thin strips

Heat the oil in a wok or frying pan, add the chicken and cook over a high heat for 5 minutes or until cooked through. Add the hoisin sauce, ginger paste and soy sauce and cook, stirring, until the sauce is sticky and coats the chicken. Remove from the heat.

Warm the pancakes in a microwave oven or in a low oven according to the instructions on the packet.

Divide the bean sprouts, spring onions and cucumber between the pancakes, top with the chicken and roll up. Serve with extra hoisin sauce for dipping.

For hoisin chicken parcels, in a large bowl, mix together 2 tablespoons hoisin sauce, ½ teaspoon ginger paste and 2 teaspoons dark soy sauce. Add 2 skinless chicken breast fillets, about 175 g (6 oz) each, thinly sliced, 4 spring onions, cut into strips, 125 g (4 oz) bean sprouts and 1 large carrot, cut into strips. Divide the mixture between 4 large squares of double-thickness greaseproof paper. Fold the paper over the filling, twisting the edges to form a parcel. Place on a baking sheet and cook in a preheated oven, 200°C (400°F), Gas Mark 6, for 20 minutes. Serve with freshly cooked noodles. **Total cooking time 30 minutes.**

smoked duck citrus salad

Serves **4**
Total cooking time **15 minutes**

2 clementines
100 g (3½ oz) **watercress**
50 g (2 oz) **walnuts**, lightly
crushed
200 g (7 oz) **smoked duck
breast**, sliced

To garnish (optional)
cress leaves
pomegranate seeds

For the dressing
2 tablespoons **walnut oil**
2 teaspoons **raspberry
vinegar**
salt and **pepper**

Cut away the peel and pith from the clementines. Cut the flesh into segments, discarding the membrane, but reserving the juice in a small bowl.

Arrange the watercress on 4 plates and sprinkle with the clementine segments and the walnuts. Top with the smoked duck slices and garnish with the cress leaves and pomegranate seeds, if liked.

Whisk the oil and vinegar for the dressing into the reserved clementine juice and season to taste. Drizzle over the salad and serve.

For warm duck, clementine & walnut salad, prepare the clementines and dressing following the recipe above. Place 2 tablespoons olive oil in a frying pan over a medium heat. Generously season 175 g (6 oz) mini duck fillets and sprinkle with ½ teaspoon Szechuan pepper. Place in the hot pan and cook for 3–4 minutes, turning once, until cooked but still slightly pink. Transfer to a warm place to rest for 10 minutes. Slice the duck fillets and scatter over the clementine segments with 50 g (2 oz) lightly crushed walnuts and a handful of pomegranate seeds. Serve drizzled with the dressing. **Total cooking time 25 minutes.**

chicken satay

Serves **4**

Total cooking time **10 minutes**

12 **ready-made chicken satay skewers**
2 x 250 g (8 oz) packets **ready-cooked Thai rice**
4 tablespoons **mayonnaise**
2 tablespoons **crunchy peanut butter**
1 teaspoon **Thai red curry paste**
2 **spring onions**, sliced

Reheat the chicken satay skewers in a microwave oven or in a hot frying pan for 2–3 minutes.

Meanwhile, reheat the rice in a microwave oven or saucepan according to the instructions on the packets.

Mix together the mayonnaise, peanut butter and Thai curry paste and pour into a small serving bowl.

Serve the chicken skewers with the rice and sauce, with the spring onions sprinkled over.

For chicken satay skewers, cut 4 skinless chicken breast fillets, about 150 g (5 oz) each, into strips and coat in a mixture of 1 tablespoon dark soy sauce, 1 teaspoon soft dark brown sugar, 1 teaspoon lemon grass paste and 1 teaspoon Thai red curry paste. Leave to marinate for 10 minutes. Thread the chicken, concertina style, on to metal or bamboo skewers presoaked in cold water for 30 minutes and place them on a foil-lined grill pan. Cook under a preheated hot grill for 5 minutes until cooked through. Meanwhile, make a peanut dipping sauce. Warm 2 tablespoons crunchy peanut butter with 1 teaspoon Thai red curry paste and 4 tablespoons coconut cream in a small saucepan. Serve the chicken skewers with the peanut sauce separately and a crisp salad. **Total cooking time 30 minutes.**

tuscan-style tarts

Serves **4**
Total cooking time **20 minutes**

375 g (12 oz) **ready-rolled
  puff pastry**
2 **tomatoes**, sliced
150 g (5 oz) **spicy tomato-
  flavoured chicken slices**
8 small pieces of **ready-
  roasted pepper**, from a jar,
  drained
1 tablespoon **thyme leaves**
125 g (4 oz) **Kalamata olives**
1 tablespoon **olive oil**
salt and **pepper**
green salad, to serve

Unroll the ready-rolled puff pastry, cut it into 4 x 12 cm (5 inch) circles and place, well spaced apart, on a large baking sheet. Prick the bases all over with a fork.

Arrange the tomato slices randomly on top of each one, dividing them evenly between the bases and keeping a 1 cm (½ inch) border around the edge. Evenly scatter over the chicken slices, peppers, thyme and olives, then drizzle with the olive oil and season to taste.

Bake at the top of a preheated oven, 220°C (425°F), Gas Mark 7, for 12–15 minutes or until the pastry is puffed and golden and the topping soft. Serve the tarts with a simple green salad.

For Tuscan tart with artichokes & lemon, unroll 375 g (12 oz) ready-rolled puff pastry on a large baking sheet. Scatter over a 400 g (13 oz) well-drained jar of artichokes mixed with the finely grated rind of 1 lemon and 4 tablespoons chopped parsley. Toss 150 g (5 oz) cooked spicy tomato chicken slices with 1 tablespoon of the artichoke oil or olive oil and scatter over the top with 1 chopped tomato and 125 g (4 oz) Kalamata olives. Bake in a preheated oven, 220°C (425°F), Gas Mark 7, for 25 minutes or until well puffed and golden. **Total cooking time 30 minutes.**

ginger & coriander turkey burgers

Serves **4**
Total cooking time **20 minutes**

450 g (14½ oz) **minced turkey**
1 tablespoon finely grated **fresh root ginger**
3 tablespoons finely chopped **fresh coriander**
50 g (2 oz) **fresh white breadcrumbs**
2 teaspoons **dark soy sauce**
2 tablespoons lightly beaten **egg**
2 tablespoons **vegetable oil**
pepper

To serve
4 tablespoons **chilli jam**
4 large or 8 small **bread rolls**, split and griddled
4–8 **lettuce leaves**

Place the turkey in a large bowl with the ginger, coriander, breadcrumbs and soy sauce. Season with pepper and add the egg, mixing well to combine. Form into 4 large or 8 small burgers.

Heat the oil in a large, nonstick frying pan and fry the burgers for 3–4 minutes on each side until cooked through and golden.

Spread the chilli jam on to the bottom halves of the griddled rolls and top with the lettuce leaves. Place a burger on top of each and cover with the top half. Serve immediately.

For baked turkey breast with ginger & coriander,
mix together 1 tablespoon finely grated fresh root ginger, 3 tablespoons finely chopped fresh coriander, 2 tablespoons chilli jam and 1 tablespoon light soy sauce in a bowl. Cut some slashes in 4 turkey breast fillet portions, about 150 g (5 oz) each, and massage in the ginger and coriander marinade. Place in an ovenproof dish and cover with foil. Cook in a preheated oven, 200°C (400°F), Gas Mark 6, for about 20 minutes until cooked through. Serve with 500 g (1 lb) cooked rice, extra chilli jam and lime wedges. **Total cooking time 30 minutes.**

Stir-fried duck with orange rice

Serves **4**

Total cooking time **20 minutes**

200 g (7 oz) **easy-cook long-grain rice**

2 tablespoons **sesame oil**

1 **red onion**, cut into slim wedges

4 **boneless, skin-on duck breasts**, about 150 g (5 oz) each, thickly sliced

1 bunch of **spring onions**, cut into 2.5 cm (1 inch) lengths

175 g (6 oz) **sugar snap peas**

finely pared rind and juice of 1 **orange**

2 tablespoons **dark soy sauce**

1 tablespoon **soft light brown sugar**

salt

Bring a large saucepan of lightly salted water to the boil and cook the rice for 12–15 minutes until tender. Drain and keep warm.

Meanwhile, heat the oil in a large wok or heavy-based frying pan over a medium-high heat and stir-fry the red onion for 5 minutes. Add the duck slices and stir-fry for 5 minutes until the duck is almost cooked. Add the spring onions and sugar snap peas and stir-fry over a high heat for 2 minutes.

Add the drained rice to the pan and toss well. Mix together the orange rind and juice, soy sauce and sugar in a small bowl, then pour over the duck mixture and toss well to distribute the sauce through the dish. Serve immediately in warmed serving bowls.

For Chinese duck noodles, heat 2 tablespoons sesame oil in a large wok or heavy-based frying pan over a medium-high heat and stir-fry 4 boneless, skin-on duck breasts, about 150 g (5 oz) each, thickly sliced, for 5 minutes. Add 1 bunch of spring onions, cut into 2.5 cm (1 inch) lengths, and 175 g (6 oz) sugar snap peas and stir-fry over a high heat for 2 minutes. Stir in 300 g (10 oz) ready-cooked Thai rice noodles and 6 tablespoons hoisin sauce and heat through for 2 minutes. **Total cooking time 15 minutes.**

butter & lemon-roasted chicken

Serves **4**
Total cooking time **30 minutes**

8 **boneless, skinless chicken
  thighs**
finely grated rind and juice of
  1 lemon
3 tablespoons chopped
  parsley
50 g (2 oz) **butter**
pepper
seasonal vegetables, to serve

Open out the chicken thighs, then put them in a large
bowl with the lemon rind and juice, parsley and plenty
of pepper. Mix well to coat the chicken. Roll each of
the coated thighs back into shape and secure with a
cocktail stick.

Put the chicken thighs in a roasting tin, pouring any
remaining juices over them, and top each with a small
knob of butter. Cook in a preheated oven, 200°C
(400°F), Gas Mark 6, for 20–25 minutes or until golden
and cooked through. Serve with seasonal vegetables.

For pan-fried thighs with lemon & butter, open out
8 boneless, skinless chicken thighs and cut in half
along each width. Place the chicken pieces in a large
bowl with the finely grated rind and juice of 1 lemon
and 3 tablespoons chopped parsley. Season with salt
and pepper and mix well. Heat 50 g (2 oz) butter in a
large, heavy-based frying pan and cook the chicken,
turning frequently, for 15 minutes or until golden and
cooked through. Serve with instant mashed potato or
rice. **Total cooking time 20 minutes.**

quick paella

Serves **4**
Total cooking time **30 minutes**

2 tablespoons **olive oil**
4 **chicken drumsticks**
75 g (3 oz) **chorizo sausage**,
  thinly sliced
1 small **red onion**, thinly sliced
200 g (7 oz) **paella rice**
900 ml (1 ½ pints) **rich
  chicken stock**
pinch of **saffron threads**
400 g (13 oz) can **artichoke
  hearts**, drained and halved
100 g (3½ oz) large **raw
  peeled prawns**
100 g (3½ oz) **green beans**,
  trimmed

Heat the oil in a large paella pan, wok or frying pan and cook the chicken drumsticks, turning occasionally, over a high heat for 5 minutes or until golden. Add the chorizo and onion to the pan and cook, stirring, for 2 minutes.

Add the rice and toss to mix. Pour in all the stock and the saffron threads, then bring to the boil. Reduce the heat, cover and simmer, stirring occasionally, for 15 minutes.

Stir in the artichokes, prawns and beans. Cook, covered, for a further 5 minutes until all the ingredients are piping hot, cooked through and tender.

For chicken, prawn & chorizo pilaf, cook 250 g (8 oz) easy-cook white rice in a large saucepan of lightly salted boiling water for 12–15 minutes or until tender, then drain. Meanwhile, heat 3 tablespoons olive oil in a large frying pan and cook 1 sliced red onion and 250 g (8 oz) diced chicken meat with 75 g (3 oz) sliced chorizo sausage for 8–10 minutes or until golden. Add a 400 g (13 oz) can artichokes, drained and halved, 100 g (3½ oz) frozen peas and 150 ml (¼ pint) chicken stock. Bring to the boil and cook for 2 minutes. Add the drained rice and toss together. Serve in warmed serving bowls with chopped parsley to garnish, if liked. **Total cooking time 20 minutes.**

polenta-crusted pork

Serves **4**
Total cooking time **30 minutes**

4 tablespoons **instant polenta**
4 tablespoons grated
  Parmesan cheese
2 tablespoons **plain flour**
1 **egg**, beaten
4 **pork loin steaks**, about
  150 g (5 oz) each
3 **pears**, cored and sliced
1 **red onion**, sliced
75 g (3 oz) **rocket leaves**
2 tablespoons **walnut pieces**
3 tablespoons **olive oil**
1 tablespoon **balsamic**
  vinegar
50 g (2 oz) **butter**

Mix together the polenta and Parmesan in a shallow bowl. Place the flour and egg in separate bowls.

Dip the pork into the flour, then the egg and finally coat with the polenta mixture. Chill for 5 minutes.

Place the pears, onion, rocket and walnuts in a bowl and toss with 2 tablespoons of the olive oil and the balsamic vinegar.

Heat the remaining oil and butter in a frying pan and cook the pork steaks for 3–4 minutes on each side until golden and cooked through.

Serve on a bed of the dressed salad.

For pork steaks with pears, heat 2 tablespoons olive oil in a roasting tin on the hob and cook 2 red onions, cut into wedges, 2 cored and quartered pears and a few sprigs of rosemary for about 10 minutes until the onions and pears are softened and well browned. Add 4 pork loin steaks, about 150 g (5 oz) each, and fry for 2–3 minutes on each side, until cooked through. Crumble over 65 g (2½ oz) Gorgonzola cheese, place the roasting tin under a preheated hot grill and cook until the cheese starts to melt. Serve with steamed green vegetables. **Total cooking time 25 minutes.**

baked lamb-stuffed aubergine

Serves **4**
Total cooking time **30 minutes**

5 tablespoons **olive or
  vegetable oil**
2 **aubergines**, about 400 g
  (13 oz) each, halved
  lengthways
1 **onion**, chopped
2 **garlic cloves**, sliced
25 g (1 oz) **pine nuts**
400 g (13 oz) **minced lamb**
2 teaspoons **ground cumin**
½ teaspoon **ground
  cinnamon**
3 tablespoons chopped **mint**
75 ml (3 fl oz) **dry white wine**
100 g (3½ oz) **feta cheese**
salt and **pepper**

To serve
steamed **couscous**
lemon wedges

Heat 3 tablespoons of the oil in a roasting tin on the hob and cook the aubergines, cut-sides down, for 5 minutes until golden, then turn and cook the other side for 2–3 minutes. Season generously and transfer, cut sides up, to a preheated oven, 200°C (400°F), Gas Mark 6, for 8–10 minutes.

Meanwhile, heat the remaining oil in a large frying pan. Add the onion and garlic and cook for 5–6 minutes. Add the pine nuts and cook for 1–2 minutes until golden.

Add the minced lamb to the pan with the cumin and cinnamon and fry over a medium-high heat, stirring frequently, for 5–6 minutes until browned. Stir in the chopped mint and season lightly.

Remove the aubergines from the oven, spoon the lamb mixture over the top and pour over the white wine. Crumble over the feta and return to the oven for a further 10 minutes until bubbling and lightly golden. Serve with lemon wedges and steamed couscous.

For griddled lamb with pine nuts, mix 5 tablespoons olive oil with 2 teaspoons ground cumin, ½ teaspoon ground cinnamon, grated rind of 1 lemon and salt and pepper, and rub into 4 lamb leg steaks, about 125 g (4 oz) each. Heat a griddle pan and cook the steaks for 3–4 minutes on each side. Scatter with 25 g (1 oz) pine nuts, 3 tablespoons chopped mint and 100 g (3½ oz) crumbled feta cheese, and serve with couscous and lemon wedges. **Total cooking time 10 minutes.**

pork chops with plum relish

Serves **4**

Total cooking time **20 minutes**

2 tablespoons **olive oil**

1 small **onion**, finely chopped

1 tablespoon grated **fresh root ginger**

4 **plums**, stoned and sliced

1 tablespoon **soft light brown sugar**

1 teaspoon **red wine vinegar**

finely grated rind of ½ **orange**

100 ml (3½ fl oz) **water**

4 **pork chops**, about 150 g (5 oz) each

salt and **pepper**

handful of **watercress**, to serve

Heat 1 tablespoon of the oil in a small saucepan, add the onion and cook for 5 minutes until softened. Add the ginger, plums, sugar, vinegar, orange rind and measurement water and simmer for 10 minutes until soft. Season to taste.

Meanwhile, rub the remaining oil over the chops and season. Cook under a preheated hot grill for 5 minutes on each side until just cooked through.

Serve with spoonfuls of the relish and the watercress.

For grilled pork with plum salsa, rub 1 tablespoon olive oil over 4 pork chops, about 150 g (5 oz) each. Season and cook under a preheated hot grill for 5 minutes on each side until golden and cooked through. Meanwhile, stone and roughly chop 3 plums and place in a small bowl. Add 1 finely chopped red chilli, the juice of ½ lime, 1 tablespoon orange juice and 2 tablespoons olive oil. Mix together and spoon the salsa over the pork chops to serve. **Total cooking time 15 minutes.**

warm tomato, liver & bacon salad

Serves **4**
Total cooking time **15 minutes**

2 tablespoons **olive oil**
150 g (5 oz) **smoked streaky bacon**, chopped
250 g (8 oz) **chicken livers**, trimmed
4 **ripe tomatoes**, sliced
125 g (4 oz) **watercress** or **lambs' lettuce**
½ **red onion**, halved and sliced
salt and **pepper**

For the dressing
3 tablespoons **olive oil**
1 tablespoon **red wine vinegar**
1 teaspoon **Dijon mustard**
pinch of **sugar**

Heat the oil in a nonstick frying pan and cook the bacon for 3–4 minutes until crisp and golden. Remove from the pan with a slotted spoon and set aside. Season the chicken livers with salt and pepper and add to the hot pan. Cook for 4–5 minutes until browned and cooked through.

Meanwhile, combine all the dressing ingredients in a jar with a tight-fitting lid and shake well.

Arrange the tomatoes on 4 plates with the watercress or lamb's lettuce and onion. Scatter the liver and bacon over the prepared salads and serve immediately, drizzled with the dressing.

For liver & bacon tagliatelle, heat 2 tablespoons olive oil in a frying pan and cook 150 g (5 oz) chopped smoked streaky bacon for 3–4 minutes. Add 1 chopped red onion and 2 chopped garlic cloves. Cook for 4–5 minutes. Meanwhile, cook 500 g (1 lb) dried tagliatelle according to the packet instructions until al dente. Add 250 g (8 oz) chicken livers, trimmed, to the frying pan and fry for 2–3 minutes to brown, then add 2 tablespoons dry sherry, scraping the bottom of the pan to loosen any bits. Add 200 ml (7 fl oz) single cream, 4 drained and chopped sundried tomatoes in oil and 1 teaspoon dried sage. Season and simmer for 2–3 minutes until the livers are just cooked. When ready, drain the tagliatelle and serve with the liver and bacon. **Total cooking time 20 minutes.**

steak with peppercorn sauce

Serves **4**

Total cooking time **10 minutes**

2 tablespoons **olive oil**

4 **feather steaks**, about 125 g
(4 oz) each

25 g (1 oz) **butter**

125 ml (4 fl oz) **single cream**

2 teaspoons **green
peppercorns in brine**,
drained

salt and **pepper**

To serve
green salad
chips or **crusty bread**

Heat the oil in a large, nonstick frying pan and fry the steaks for 1–3 minutes on each side, depending on how you like your steak. Season to taste with salt and pepper, remove the steaks from the pan and transfer to a warm ovenproof dish to rest.

Add the butter, cream and peppercorns to the pan, and bubble over a medium-low heat for 1–2 minutes, scraping the pan to loosen any tasty bits.

Serve the steaks drizzled with the sauce, accompanied by green salad and chips or bread.

For green peppercorn burgers with blue cheese sauce, place 400 g (13 oz) minced beef in a bowl with 1 chopped red onion, 2 teaspoons drained green peppercorns in brine, 25 g (1 oz) ready-made natural dried breadcrumbs, 1 beaten egg and 1 tablespoon finely chopped parsley or chives, then season and mix to combine. Form into 4 burgers. Heat 2 tablespoons olive oil in a frying pan and cook the burgers for 4–5 minutes on each side until cooked through. Meanwhile, place 100 g (3½ oz) creamy blue cheese in a small bowl with 2 tablespoons crème fraîche and lots of pepper. Mash together until smooth. Serve on buns with the burgers and some slices of fresh tomato. **Total cooking time 20 minutes.**

grilled tandoori lamb chops

Serves **4**

Total cooking time **20 minutes**

8 **lamb loin chops** or **cutlets**,
about 85 g (3¼ oz) each
3 **garlic cloves**, finely grated
1 teaspoon finely grated **fresh
root ginger**
juice of 2 large **lemons**
1 tablespoon **ground cumin**
3 tablespoons **tandoori curry
paste**
250 ml (8 fl oz) **natural yogurt**
vegetable oil, for oiling
salt and **pepper**
chopped **mint leaves**,
to garnish

To serve
cucumber salad
mini naan breads

Put the lamb in a single layer in a shallow, non-metallic dish. Mix together the remaining ingredients, except the oil, in a bowl, then season well. Pour the mixture over the lamb, toss to coat evenly, then cover and leave to marinate for 10 minutes.

Place the lamb on a lightly oiled grill rack and cook under a preheated hot grill for 2–3 minutes on each side or until cooked to your liking.

Transfer on to 4 warmed serving plates, scatter with chopped mint and serve with cucumber salad and mini naan breads.

For tandoori roast rack of lamb, mix together 3 tablespoons tandoori curry paste and 100 ml (3½ fl oz) Greek yogurt in a bowl. Using a small, sharp knife, make deep slashes in the meat of 2 French-trimmed racks of lamb (with about 7–8 ribs each). Season well, then spread the tandoori mixture all over the lamb. Put the racks, rib-side up, on a nonstick baking sheet and place in a preheated oven, 180°C (350°F), Gas Mark 4, for 15–20 minutes or until cooked to your liking. Cover with foil and leave to rest for a few minutes before serving. **Total cooking time 30 minutes.**

beef & peppercorn stroganoff

Serves **4**

Total cooking time **15 minutes**

25 g (1 oz) **butter**

1 **red onion**, thinly sliced

250 g (8 oz) **button mushrooms**, halved

3 tablespoons **tomato purée**

2 teaspoons **Dijon mustard**

1 tablespoon **pink peppercorns in brine**, drained

1 tablespoon **green peppercorns in brine**, drained

1 teaspoon **smoked paprika**

300 ml (½ pint) hot **beef stock**

500 g (1 lb) **beef fillet**, cut into thin strips

200 ml (7 fl oz) **soured cream**

salt and **pepper**

2 tablespoons chopped **flat leaf parsley**, to garnish

steamed **rice**, to serve

Heat a frying pan until hot, then add half the butter. When foaming, add the red onion and fry for 2–3 minutes or until just softened. Add the mushrooms, tomato purée, mustard, pink and green peppercorns and paprika and fry, stirring, for a further 1–2 minutes. Pour in the hot stock and bring to the boil, then reduce the heat to low and simmer for 1–2 minutes.

Meanwhile, heat a separate frying pan and add the remaining butter. Season the beef. When the butter is foaming, add the beef and cook, stirring, for 2–3 minutes or until browned all over.

Add the soured cream and beef to the onion and mushroom mixture and mix well, then season to taste.

Spoon into warmed bowls, scatter over the parsley and serve with steamed rice.

For cheat's spiced beef & mushroom pie, use the cooked beef and mushroom mixture from the above recipe to fill 4 individual pie dishes. Top each with 200 g (7 oz) ready-cooked mashed potato and place under a hot grill for 3–4 minutes or until golden. Serve with a salad. **Total cooking time 25 minutes.**

lamb cutlets with pea mash

Serves **4**

Total cooking time **20 minutes**

750 g (1½ lb) **potatoes**,
  peeled and chopped
350 g (11½ oz) **fresh** or
  frozen peas
1 tablespoon chopped
  rosemary
8 **lamb cutlets**, about 85 g
  (3¼ oz) each
30 g (1 oz) **butter**
salt and **pepper**

Cook the potatoes in a saucepan of boiling water for
12–15 minutes until tender, adding the peas 2 minutes
before the end of the cooking time.

Meanwhile, sprinkle half the rosemary over the lamb
cutlets then cook them under a preheated hot grill for
3–4 minutes on each side or until cooked to your liking.
Leave to rest.

Drain the potatoes and peas, then return to the pan
and lightly mash with the remaining rosemary, butter
and salt and pepper to taste. Serve the lamb cutlets
accompanied by the pea and rosemary mash.

For lamb racks with rosemary & garlic, cut small
slits into 4 x 3-cutlet racks of lamb and insert 2 sliced
garlic cloves and 4 rosemary sprigs into the slits. Whisk
together 1 tablespoon clear honey, 2 tablespoons
wholegrain mustard and 1 tablespoon ready-made
mint sauce in a bowl, then brush over the lamb. Leave
to marinate at room temperature for 10 minutes. Place
in a roasting tin and cook in a preheated oven, 200°C
(400°F), Gas Mark 6, for 18 minutes or until cooked
to your liking, basting with the marinade 2 or 3 times.
Serve the lamb with griddled asparagus and mashed
potato. **Total cooking time 30 minutes.**

creamy veal escalopes

Serves **4**

Total cooking time **30 minutes**

10 g (⅓ oz) **dried porcini
mushrooms**

4 **veal escalopes**, about
150 g (5 oz) each

2 tablespoons **plain flour**

50 g (2 oz) **butter**

1 tablespoon **olive oil**

2 **garlic cloves**, chopped

1 **onion**, chopped

100 g (3½ oz) **chestnut
mushrooms**, trimmed and
sliced

100 ml (3½ fl oz) **white wine**

200 ml (7 fl oz) **single cream**

large handful of **baby spinach
leaves**

salt and **pepper**

mashed potato, to serve

Soak the porcini in just enough boiling water to cover
for 10 minutes. Drain, reserving the liquid, and roughly
chop the porcini.

Dust the veal escalopes with the flour. Heat the butter
and the olive oil in a frying pan and cook the escalopes
for 2–3 minutes on each side until just cooked through.
Remove from the pan and keep warm.

Add the garlic, onion and chestnut mushrooms to the
pan and sauté for 4–5 minutes until the onion is soft.

Pour in the wine and bubble for 2–3 minutes, then
pour in the cream and 2–3 tablespoons of the reserved
porcini liquid.

Bring to the boil, then stir in the porcini and spinach
and season to taste with salt and pepper. Return the
escalopes to the pan and cook for 1 minute before
serving with mashed potatoes.

For veal salad, heat 1 tablespoon olive oil in a frying
pan and cook a 300 g (10 oz) veal steak for 1–2
minutes on each side or until cooked to your liking.
Rest for 1–2 minutes, then slice thinly against the grain.
In a large salad bowl, toss the veal with 2 chopped beef
tomatoes, 50 g (2 oz) bistro salad leaves, 20 g (¾ oz)
rocket leaves, 2 tablespoons chopped walnuts and
75 g (3 oz) drained and sliced ready-roasted peppers
from a jar. Serve dressed with 2–3 tablespoons Italian
salad dressing and sprinkled with 3 tablespoons
Parmesan cheese shavings. **Total cooking time
15 minutes.**

harissa beef fajitas

Serves **4**
Total cooking time **15 minutes**

3 teaspoons **harissa paste**
½ teaspoon **paprika**
2 tablespoons **olive oil**
525 g (1 lb 2 oz) **rump steak**,
  cut into thick strips
8 **tortilla wraps**
½ **iceburg lettuce**, shredded
4 tablespoons **soured cream**
4 tablespoons **ready-made**
  guacamole
4 tablespoons **ready-made**
  tomato salsa
4 tablespoons grated
  Cheddar cheese

Mix together the harissa, paprika and oil in a non-metallic bowl. Add the steak and mix to coat, then cover and leave to marinate for 5 minutes.

Heat a griddle pan until hot, add the steak and cook for 20 seconds on each side or until cooked to your liking. Remove from the pan and keep warm.

Warm the tortillas in a microwave oven according to the instructions on the packet. Sprinkle some shredded lettuce in the centre of each tortilla and layer the steak on top. Spoon a little soured cream, guacamole and salsa over the steak, then sprinkle over the cheese. Roll up the wraps and serve.

For harissa beef burgers, place 525 g (1 lb 2 oz) minced beef, 2 tablespoons chopped fresh coriander, 1 tablespoon harissa paste, 1 chopped onion, 1 egg yolk, 1 tablespoon olive oil and salt and pepper in a food processor and blend together. Shape into 4 equal-sized burgers, cover and chill for 10 minutes. Cook the burgers under a preheated medium grill for 15 minutes, turning once. Meanwhile, toast 4 halved burger buns. Place a burger on each base and top with shredded iceburg lettuce, sliced tomatoes, sliced red onion and a dollop of mayonnaise or soured cream. Top with the lids and serve. **Total cooking time 30 minutes.**

lamb & olive stew

Serves **4**

Total cooking time **30 minutes**

450 g (14½ oz) **boneless shoulder of lamb**, cut into small cubes

2 tablespoons **plain flour**, seasoned

2 tablespoons **olive oil**

1 **onion**, chopped

2 **carrots**, peeled and diced

2 **garlic cloves**, chopped

½ tablespoon chopped **rosemary**

200 ml (7 fl oz) **white wine**

400 g (13 oz) can **chopped tomatoes**

12 **black olives**, pitted

grated rind and juice of 1 **lemon**

2 tablespoons chopped **parsley**

900 ml (1½ pints) **water**

200 g (7 oz) **instant polenta**

25 g (1 oz) **butter**

2 tablespoons grated **Parmesan cheese**

Dust the cubes of lamb with the seasoned flour. Heat the olive oil in a saucepan and brown the meat all over.

Add the onion and cook for 3 minutes, stirring, then add the carrots, garlic and rosemary and cook for a further 3–4 minutes until the vegetables are softened.

Pour in the white wine and chopped tomatoes, bring to the boil and then simmer for 20 minutes until the lamb is tender.

Stir in the olives, lemon rind and juice and chopped parsley 1 minute before the end of cooking.

Meanwhile, bring the measurement water to the boil in another saucepan and pour in the polenta. Cook, stirring continuously, for 1 minute. Stir in the butter and grated Parmesan and divide between 4 bowls.

Spoon the lamb stew over the polenta and serve.

For lamb cutlets with fried polenta, heat 2 tablespoons olive oil in a frying pan and fry 8 slices of ready-made polenta for 2 minutes on each side. Remove and keep warm. Add 1 tablespoon olive oil to the same pan and fry 1 finely diced onion and 1 finely diced red chilli for 1 minute before adding 8 lamb cutlets, about 85 g (3¼ oz) each, and a sprinkling of dried oregano. Cook the lamb for 2 minutes on each side. Sprinkle in a dash of red wine and 2 tablespoons chopped pitted black olives. Serve the cutlets with the fried polenta. **Total cooking time 15 minutes.**

gammon steaks with apricot sauce

Serves **4**

Total cooking time **25 minutes**

500 g (1 lb) **potatoes**, peeled
and cut into cubes

4 **lean gammon steaks**, about
100 g (3½ oz) each

3 tablespoons **vegetable oil**

1 **onion**, roughly chopped

400 g (13 oz) can **apricots in
fruit juice**, drained and juice
reserved

1 teaspoon **ground cinnamon**

2 teaspoons **paprika**

3 tablespoons chopped
parsley

salt and **pepper**

Bring a large saucepan of lightly salted water to the
boil and cook the potatoes for 10 minutes. Drain.

Meanwhile, cook the gammon under a preheated hot
grill for 5–6 minutes on each side until cooked through.

While the potatoes and gammon are cooking, heat
1 tablespoon of the oil in a large, heavy-based
saucepan and cook the onion over a medium heat,
stirring frequently, for 3–4 minutes until softened. Add
the apricot juice and cinnamon and cook over a high
heat for 3 minutes to reduce the liquid by half. Remove
from the heat and add the apricots, then pour all the
mixture into a food processor or blender and whizz to a
thick, textured sauce. Return to the saucepan and heat
through gently while finishing the potatoes.

Heat the remaining oil in a large, heavy-based frying
pan and cook the drained potatoes over a high heat,
stirring frequently, for 5 minutes until golden and crisp.
Sprinkle over the paprika, season with pepper and toss
in the parsley.

Spoon the sauce over the gammon to serve,
accompanied by the paprika potatoes.

For spiced apricot-glazed gammon, warm 2
tablespoons apricot jam in a small saucepan, then stir
in ½ teaspoon ground cumin and season with pepper.
Cook 4 lean gammon steaks, about 100 g (3½ oz)
each, under a preheated hot grill, brushing frequently
with the glaze, for 5–6 minutes on each side until
cooked through. Serve with a tub of ready-prepared
Moroccan couscous. **Total cooking time 10 minutes.**

pan-fried gnocchi & chorizo salad

Serves **4**
Total cooking time **15 minutes**

2 tablespoons **olive oil**
400 g (13 oz) **ready-made gnocchi**
4 large, **ripe tomatoes**, roughly chopped
1 small bunch of **basil leaves**, roughly shredded
125 g (4 oz) **mozzarella cheese**, torn into pieces
100 g (3½ oz) sliced **chorizo sausage**
1–2 tablespoons **balsamic vinegar**
salt and **pepper**

Heat the olive oil in a large, nonstick frying pan and add the gnocchi. Pan-fry for about 8 minutes, moving frequently, until crisp and golden.

Meanwhile, toss the tomatoes with the shredded basil and torn mozzarella, season to taste and arrange on 4 serving plates.

Add the chorizo to the pan of gnocchi for the final 1–2 minutes of cooking until slightly crisp and golden.

Scatter the gnocchi and chorizo over the salads, and serve drizzled with the balsamic vinegar.

For creamy gnocchi & chorizo bake, dice 4 large tomatoes and place in a large bowl with 100 g (3½ oz) sliced chorizo sausage, 750 g (1½ lb) ready-made gnocchi, 1 small bunch of basil leaves, roughly shredded, and 1–2 tablespoons balsamic vinegar. Season generously, then tip into a large ovenproof dish, pour over 150 ml (¼ pint) single cream and scatter with 125 g (4 oz) mozzarella cheese, torn into pieces. Cook in a preheated oven, 200°C (400°F), Gas Mark 6, for about 20 minutes until bubbling and golden. Serve with plenty of mixed salad leaves. **Total cooking time 30 minutes.**

rack of lamb with harissa

Serves **4**
Total cooking time **30 minutes**

125 g (4 oz) **hazelnuts**
75 g (3 oz) **sesame seeds**
2 tablespoons **coriander seeds**
1 tablespoon **cumin seeds**
4 tablespoons **olive oil**
2 **racks of lamb**, about 7–8 ribs each
2 **red peppers**, cored, deseeded and thickly sliced
2 tablespoons **harissa paste**
5 tablespoons **natural yogurt**
salt and **pepper**
couscous, to serve (optional)

Put the nuts and spices in a small, dry frying pan and toast for 1 minute. Transfer to a mortar and crush roughly with a pestle, adding a little salt.

Rub 2 tablespoons of the oil over the lamb racks, season well and press the nut mixture on to the fatty side of each rack. Transfer to a shallow roasting tin and roast in a preheated oven, 220°C (425°F), Gas Mark 7, for 10 minutes. Arrange the peppers around the lamb and return to the oven for a further 10–15 minutes for rare to medium lamb.

Swirl the harissa over the yogurt in a bowl. Slice the lamb racks and serve with the peppers, drizzling over the harissa sauce. Serve with couscous, if liked.

For easy spiced lamb pilaf, heat 1 tablespoon olive oil in a flameproof casserole, add 1 tablespoon harissa paste and then 325 g (11 oz) lamb leg chunks. Stir around the pan until well coated, then stir in 300 g (10 oz) basmati rice. Pour over 600 ml (1 pint) chicken stock and bring to the boil. Leave to simmer, uncovered, for 10 minutes. Stir in 150 g (5 oz) baby spinach leaves, reduce the heat to low, cover and cook for a further 5 minutes until the rice is tender. Sprinkle with mint leaves and drizzle with natural yogurt to serve. **Total cooking time 20 minutes.**

fish & seafood

stuffed mussels

Serves **4**

Total cooking time **30 minutes**

1–1.5 kg (2–3 lb) large
live mussels (about 48
mussels), scrubbed and
debearded

65 g (2½ oz) **fresh white
breadcrumbs**

50 g (2 oz) **walnut pieces**

200 g (7 oz) **butter**

6 **garlic cloves**, chopped

juice of 1 **lemon**

2 tablespoons grated
Parmesan cheese

2 tablespoons chopped
tarragon

small handful of **parsley**,
chopped

Put the mussels in a large saucepan, discarding any
that are cracked or don't shut when tapped, cover and
steam for 5 minutes, shaking the pan occasionally, until
they have opened, then drain. Discard any that remain
closed. Break off the empty half of the shells and place
the mussels on a large baking sheet.

Place the breadcrumbs, walnuts, butter, garlic, lemon
juice and grated Parmesan in a food processor and blitz
until the mixture starts to come together. Add the herbs
and blend until combined.

Divide the herb mixture between the mussels, making
sure each mussel is covered. Cook under a preheated
hot grill for 2–3 minutes until the stuffing is golden. You
may need to cook the mussels in batches if you cannot
fit them all on the baking sheet at once.

Serve immediately.

For smoked mussel bruschetta, toast 8 slices of
ciabatta on both sides, then rub each slice with a garlic
clove. Roughly chop 200 g (7 oz) smoked mussels and
mix with 2 roughly chopped tomatoes, 1 tablespoon
chopped parsley and the juice of ½ lemon. Spoon the
mussel mixture on to the toast and serve topped with
a few rocket leaves. **Total cooking time 10 minutes.**

halibut ceviche with grapefruit

Serves **2**
Total cooking time **25 minutes**

450 g (14½ oz) **skinless halibut fillet**
2 **limes**
1 **grapefruit**
100 g (3½ oz) **cherry tomatoes**, halved
1 **red chilli**, deseeded (optional) and sliced
handful of **mint**, finely sliced
1 tablespoon **extra virgin olive oil**
salt and **pepper**

Using a very sharp knife, cut the fish into thin slices.

Grate the rind from 1 lime into a non-metallic bowl, then squeeze in the juice from both limes. Cut off the base of the grapefruit, then cut around the flesh to remove the rind and pith. Slice into segments and set aside. Add any juice from the grapefruit to the bowl.

Add the fish to the lime and grapefruit juices and toss to coat. Cover and leave to marinate in the refrigerator for 15 minutes.

Discard the marinade from the fish. Arrange the fish on a serving plate with the grapefruit segments and tomatoes. Scatter over the chilli and mint, season and drizzle with the oil to serve.

For spicy halibut & grapefruit salad, mix together 1 tablespoon vegetable oil, ½ finely chopped red chilli and a handful of fresh coriander, finely chopped. Toss with 450 g (14½ oz) skinless halibut fillet, cut into bite-sized pieces. Cook under a preheated hot grill for 2–3 minutes on each side. Meanwhile, peel 3 segments of grapefruit and cut into small pieces. Whisk together 1 tablespoon vegetable oil and 1 tablespoon rice vinegar. Toss with 100 g (3½ oz) mixed salad leaves and another handful of coriander leaves, top with the grapefruit and halibut and serve. **Total cooking time 15 minutes.**

prawn & avocado tostada

Serves **4**

Total cooking time **10 minutes**

4 large **soft flour tortillas**

1 small **iceberg lettuce**, shredded

300 g (10 oz) **cooked peeled prawns**

1 large, **ripe but firm avocado**, stoned, peeled and diced

2 tablespoons chopped **fresh coriander**

1 tablespoon **lime juice**

salt and **cracked black pepper**

lime wedges, to serve

Heat a griddle pan and toast a tortilla for 30–60 seconds on each side until lightly charred. Immediately push it into a small, deep bowl and set aside. Repeat with the remaining tortillas to make 4 bowl-shaped tortillas. Place one-quarter of the shredded lettuce inside each one.

Meanwhile, toss together the prawns, avocado, coriander and lime juice, and season to taste.

Divide the prawn and avocado mixture between the tortillas and serve with lime wedges for squeezing over.

For prawn & black bean chilli, heat 2 tablespoons vegetable oil in a large frying pan and add 4 chopped spring onions, 2 chopped garlic cloves and 1 finely deseeded and chopped red chilli. Cook gently for 2 minutes until softened, then add a 400 g (13 oz) can chopped tomatoes and a 400 g (13 oz) can black beans, rinsed and drained. Simmer gently for 10–12 minutes until thickened slightly. Stir in 3 tablespoons chopped fresh coriander, 1 tablespoon lime juice and 250 g (8 oz) cooked peeled prawns. Simmer for 1 minute until the prawns are hot, and serve with griddled tortillas and lime wedges, scattered with extra coriander. **Total cooking time 25 minutes.**

manhattan clam chowder

Serves **4**

Total cooking time **30 minutes**

1 tablespoon **vegetable oil**
125 g (4 oz) **lardons**
1 large **onion**, chopped
1 **celery stick**, chopped
1 **carrot**, peeled and chopped
3 **potatoes**, peeled and
   chopped
400 g (13 oz) can **tomatoes**
1 **thyme sprig**
1.5 litres (2½ pints) **fish stock**
500 g (1 lb) **live clams**,
   scrubbed
125 ml (4 fl oz) **dry white
wine**
salt and **pepper**
crusty bread or **crackers**, to
   serve (optional)

Heat the oil in a large saucepan, add the lardons and cook for 2 minutes until browned. Stir in the onion, celery and carrot and cook for a further 5 minutes until softened.

Add the potatoes, tomatoes, thyme and stock. Cook for 12–15 minutes until the potatoes are soft.

Meanwhile, put the clams in a large saucepan, discarding any that are cracked or don't shut when tapped. Add the wine, cover and cook for 5 minutes or until the clams have opened. Discard any that remain closed. Remove the clam meat from most of the shells, keeping some in their shells for decoration, and reserve the juice.

Season the chowder and add the clam meat, whole clams and clam juice to the pan. Heat through and serve with crusty bread or crackers, if liked.

For clam & tomato linguine, heat 1 tablespoon olive oil in a large saucepan, add 2 crushed garlic cloves and cook for 30 seconds. Add 125 ml (4 fl oz) dry white wine and 400 g (13 oz) scrubbed live clams, discarding any that are cracked or don't shut when tapped. Cover and cook for 5 minutes, shaking the pan occasionally, or until the clams have opened. Discard any that remain closed. Stir in 1 tablespoon lemon juice and 150 g (5 oz) halved cherry tomatoes. Cook 500 g (1 lb) fresh linguine according to the packet instructions until al dente, then drain, reserving a little cooking water. Stir into the clams with 25 g (1 oz) butter and the reserved pasta cooking water if needed. Scatter over some chopped parsley and serve. **Total cooking time 15 minutes.**

sesame tuna with ginger dressing

Serves **6**

Total cooking time **25 minutes**

875 g (1¾ lb) piece of **fresh tuna**

2 tablespoons **vegetable oil**

3 tablespoons **white sesame seeds**

3 tablespoons **black sesame seeds**

½ **cucumber**, sliced into ribbons

2 **avocados**, stoned, peeled and sliced

2 **spring onions**, shredded

salt and **pepper**

For the dressing

1 **garlic clove**, crushed

1 **chilli**, deseeded and finely chopped

1 teaspoon finely chopped **fresh root ginger**

1 tablespoon **soy sauce**

juice of ½ **lime**

1 teaspoon grated **orange rind**

1 tablespoon **clear honey**

1 tablespoon **sesame oil**

Season the tuna. Heat the oil in a large frying pan, add the tuna and cook for 3–5 minutes or until browned all over.

Spread the sesame seeds on a plate and press the seared tuna into them until well coated. Put on a baking sheet and cook in a preheated oven, 220°C (425°F), Gas Mark 7, for 10–12 minutes until browned but still pink inside.

Mix together the ingredients for the dressing. Cut the tuna into thick slices and arrange on serving plates with the cucumber and avocado slices and spring onions. Drizzle over the dressing to serve.

For tuna carpaccio with ginger salad, cut 625 g (1¼ lb) fresh tuna into 1 cm (½ inch) steaks, put between 2 pieces of clingfilm and pound gently until thin. Arrange on serving plates. Whisk together the juice of 1 orange and 1 lime and 1 teaspoon each finely chopped fresh root ginger, rice vinegar and soy sauce. Toss through 200 g (7 oz) rocket leaves and 150 g (5 oz) sliced radishes. Arrange on top of the tuna and sprinkle with toasted sesame seeds. **Total cooking time 10 minutes.**

mixed seafood casserole

Serves **4**

Total cooking time **20 minutes**

4 tablespoons **olive oil**
1 **onion**, diced
4 **garlic cloves**, crushed
100 ml (3½ fl oz) **white wine**
400 g (13 oz) can **chopped tomatoes**
200 ml (7 fl oz) **fish stock**
pinch of **saffron threads**
400 g (13 oz) pack **ready-cooked mixed seafood**
2 tablespoons chopped **parsley**
crusty bread, to serve (optional)

Heat the olive oil in a heavy-based saucepan and sauté the onion and garlic for 3–4 minutes. Pour in the white wine and boil for 2–3 minutes, then add the chopped tomatoes, fish stock and saffron.

Bring to a simmer, stir in the mixed seafood and parsley and cook for 5–6 minutes to heat through.

Serve with crusty bread, if liked.

For seafood risotto, heat 2 tablespoons olive oil in a saucepan and sauté 1 diced onion, 1 finely diced red chilli and 2 crushed garlic cloves for 2–3 minutes. Stir in 350 g (11½ oz) Arborio risotto rice and 2 tablespoons tomato purée and cook, stirring, for 1–2 minutes. Pour in 100 ml (3½ fl oz) white wine and cook for 1–2 minutes until it is absorbed. Add a ladleful from a saucepan containing about 1 litre (1¾ pints) hot fish stock and cook, stirring continuously, until it has all been absorbed. Repeat with the remaining hot stock, adding a ladleful at a time, until the rice is al dente. Stir in a 400 g (13 oz) pack ready-cooked mixed seafood and a small handful of chopped parsley and cook for 2–3 minutes or until the seafood is heated through. Squeeze in the juice of ½ lemon and serve immediately. **Total cooking time 30 minutes.**

chilli spaghetti vongole

Serves **4**
Total cooking time **20 minutes**

450 g (14½ oz) **dried
  spaghetti**
6 tablespoons **extra virgin
  olive oil**, plus extra to serve
2 **garlic cloves**, chopped
2 **red chillies**, deseeded and
  finely chopped
4 **anchovy fillets in oil**,
  drained and chopped
small handful of **flat leaf
  parsley**, finely chopped
1 kg (2lb) **live clams**,
  scrubbed
100 ml (3½ fl oz) **dry white
  wine**
salt and **pepper**

Cook the pasta according to the packet instructions until al dente. Drain, then return to the pan.

Meanwhile, heat the oil in a frying pan, add the garlic, red chillies, anchovies and half the parsley and fry gently for a couple of minutes. Add the clams to the pan, discarding any that are cracked or don't shut when tapped. Pour in the wine, cover and cook over a medium heat for 5 minutes, shaking the pan occasionally, or until the clams have opened. Discard any that remain closed.

Add the clams and the juices to the spaghetti with the remaining parsley, then season and toss to mix well. Divide into warmed bowls, drizzle with a little extra oil and serve immediately.

For chilli & garlic-braised clams, heat 2 tablespoons olive oil in a heavy-based saucepan, add 4 chopped shallots and cook over a medium heat, stirring occasionally, for 6–8 minutes until softened. Add 2 crushed garlic cloves and 2 deseeded and finely chopped red chillies and cook, stirring, for 1–2 minutes. Stir in 2 tablespoons tomato purée and 4 finely chopped plum tomatoes and cook for a further 8–10 minutes. Add 500 ml (17 fl oz) hot fish stock and 875 g (1¾ lb) scrubbed live clams, discarding any that are cracked or don't shut when tapped, then bring to the boil, cover and cook over a medium heat for 5 minutes or until the clams have opened. Discard any that remain closed. Season, ladle into warmed bowls and serve. **Total cooking time 30 minutes.**

salt-baked bream

Serves **4**

Total cooking time **30 minutes**

2 kg (4 lb) **coarse salt**

1 tablespoon **fennel seeds**

2 **egg whites**, lightly beaten

2 **sea bream**, gutted and scaled

1 **lemon**

1 **lime**

1 **orange**

½ **fennel bulb**, trimmed and thinly sliced

4 tablespoons **extra virgin olive oil**

handful of **chives**, chopped

salt and **pepper**

Mix together the coarse salt and fennel seeds in a bowl, then stir through the egg whites. Spread about one-third of this mixture over a baking sheet or the bottom of a large ovenproof dish. Place the fish on top, then cover with the remaining salt mixture, making sure you don't have any gaps, although it's fine for the tails to be showing. Bake in a preheated oven, 200°C (400°F), Gas Mark 6, for 20 minutes.

Meanwhile, cut the peel from the citrus fruits using a sharp knife. Divide the fruits into segments by cutting between the membranes, holding them over a bowl to catch the juice. Place in the bowl with the juice, add the remaining ingredients and season.

Crack open the salt crust by giving it a sharp tap with the back of a heavy knife. Peel away the salt crust, remove the fish and serve with the dressed citrus segments and fennel alongside.

For sea bream baked on salt, spread 1 kg (2 lb) coarse salt over a baking sheet. Trim and thinly slice 1 fennel bulb and place on top of the salt together with some thyme sprigs. Lay 4 sea bream fillets on top, skin-side up, and bake in a preheated oven, 200°C (400°F), Gas Mark 6, for 10–12 minutes until the fish just starts to flake. Carefully lift the fish off the salt, squeeze over a little lemon juice and serve. **Total cooking time 20 minutes.**

mackerel with roasted tomatoes

Serves **4**

Total cooking time **30 minutes**

12 **plum tomatoes**, halved

3 tablespoons **olive oil**, plus extra for oiling

1 teaspoon **caster sugar**

1 teaspoon **red wine vinegar**

4 **mackerel fillets**, about 150 g (5 oz) each

150 ml (¼ pint) **crème fraîche**

1–2 tablespoons **horseradish sauce**

75 g (3 oz) **rocket leaves**

salt and **pepper**

Place the tomatoes on a lightly oiled baking sheet. Drizzle over 2 tablespoons of the oil, then sprinkle each tomato half with the sugar and vinegar. Place in a preheated oven, 200°C (400°F), Gas Mark 6, for 20–25 minutes until browned and soft.

Meanwhile, heat a large, dry frying pan until hot. Rub the remaining oil over the mackerel and season well. Add the mackerel to the pan, skin-side down, and cook for 5 minutes until the skin is golden. Turn over and cook for a further 3 minutes or until the fish is cooked through.

Stir together the crème fraîche and horseradish sauce.

Arrange the rocket, roasted tomatoes and mackerel on serving plates and serve with spoonfuls of the horseradish sauce on the side.

For mackerel & sunblush tomato salad, gently toss together 100 g (3½ oz) drained canned mackerel in olive oil, 75 g (3 oz) drained sunblush tomatoes and 100 g (3½ oz) rocket leaves. Whisk together the juice of ½ lemon, 3 tablespoons olive oil and 1 tablespoon horseradish sauce. Drizzle over the salad to serve. **Total cooking time 10 minutes.**

honey mustard salmon

Serves **4**
Total cooking time **10 minutes**

4 **salmon fillets**, about 150 g
(5 oz) each
olive oil, for oiling
2 tablespoons **wholegrain
mustard**
2 tablespoons **clear honey**
handful of **dill**, chopped
salt and **pepper**

To serve (optional)
new potatoes
cucumber salad

Place the salmon in a lightly oiled baking tin and season. Mix together the mustard, honey and dill and drizzle over the salmon.

Roast in a preheated oven, 220°C (425°F), Gas Mark 7, for 8 minutes or until cooked through.

Serve with some new potatoes and a cucumber salad, if liked.

For salmon with mustard Hollandaise, place 4 thin salmon fillets, about 125 g (4 oz) each, on a lightly oiled baking sheet, drizzle over 2 tablespoons olive oil and season. Place in a preheated oven, 120°C (250°F), Gas Mark ½, for 25–30 minutes until just cooked through. Meanwhile, for the sauce, crack 2 egg yolks into a heatproof bowl set snugly over a saucepan of simmering water. Add a squeeze of lemon juice and then slowly whisk in 100 g (3½ oz) melted butter until the sauce has thickened. Stir in 1 teaspoon wholegrain mustard and more lemon juice to taste. Serve with the salmon. **Total cooking time 30 minutes.**

clams in black bean sauce

Serves **4**

Total cooking time **10 minutes**

2 tablespoons **vegetable oil**
2 **spring onions**
2 **garlic cloves**, crushed
2 teaspoons finely chopped
  fresh root ginger
1 **red chilli**, finely chopped
1 tablespoon **ready-made**
  black bean sauce
1 kg (2 lb) **live clams**,
  scrubbed
3 tablespoons **chicken stock**
1 tablespoon **soy sauce**
1 tablespoon **Shaoxing wine**
fresh coriander leaves,
  to garnish

Heat the oil in a large saucepan over a high heat. Meanwhile, slice the spring onions and separate the white and green parts. Add the white spring onion, garlic, ginger and chilli to the pan and cook briefly until sizzling. Stir in the black bean sauce, then add the clams, discarding any that are cracked or don't shut when tapped, along with the remaining ingredients.

Cover the pan and cook over a medium heat for 5 minutes, shaking the pan occasionally, or until the clams have opened. Discard any that remain closed.

Divide the clams on to serving plates and scatter over the green spring onion and coriander leaves to serve.

For mussels in black bean sauce, rinse 1 tablespoon fermented black beans. Mash with a little sugar. Briefly cook 2 sliced spring onions, 2 crushed garlic cloves and 2 teaspoons each finely chopped fresh root ginger and red chilli in 2 tablespoons hot vegetable oil in a saucepan. Add the beans, 3 tablespoons chicken stock and 2 tablespoons each soy sauce and Shaoxing wine. Bring to the boil, then simmer for 5 minutes. Meanwhile, heat 2 tablespoons vegetable oil in a large saucepan. Add 1 kg (2 lb) scrubbed live mussels, discarding any that are cracked or don't shut when tapped, along with 3 tablespoons hot water. Cover and cook over a medium heat for 5 minutes, shaking the pan occasionally, or until opened. Discard any that remain closed and the top shells. Drizzle over the sauce. **Total cooking time 20 minutes.**

creamy scallops with leeks

Serves **4**
Total cooking time **15 minutes**

50 g (2 oz) **butter**
16 **shelled and cleaned
  scallops,** halved
1 **rindless streaky bacon
  rasher,** roughly snipped
3 **leeks,** trimmed, cleaned and
  sliced
200 ml (7 fl oz) **crème fraîche**
finely grated rind of **1 lemon**
pepper
quick-cook long-grain rice,
  to serve

Melt half the butter in a large, heavy-based frying pan and cook the scallops and bacon over a high heat, stirring frequently, for about 2 minutes until just golden and cooked through. Remove with a slotted spoon and keep warm.

Add the remaining butter to the pan and cook the leeks over a medium heat, stirring occasionally, for 5 minutes until softened and lightly browned in places. Add the crème fraîche and lemon rind and season generously with pepper.

Return the scallops to the pan and toss into the creamy leeks. Serve immediately with quick-cook rice.

For scallop & bacon kebabs with leeks, cut 10 smoked streaky bacon rashers in half and wrap each around 20 shelled and cleaned small scallops. Thread on to 4 metal skewers. Mix 2 tablespoons olive oil with 1 tablespoon clear honey and brush over the bacon. Melt 25 g (1 oz) butter with 1 tablespoon olive oil in a frying pan and cook 2 trimmed, cleaned and finely sliced leeks, stirring, for 6–8 minutes until soft and golden. Add 1 teaspoon each finely grated lemon rind and wholegrain mustard and 200 ml (7 fl oz) crème fraîche and heat for 2 minutes. Keep warm. Heat a griddle pan over a high heat and cook the skewers for 2–3 minutes on each side until brown and cooked through. Serve on a bed of the creamy leeks. **Total cooking time 30 minutes.**

swordfish with salsa verde

Serves **4**

Total cooking time **20 minutes**

1 ½ teaspoons **Dijon mustard**
450 ml (¾ pint) **extra virgin
   olive oil**
4 **anchovy fillets in oil**,
   drained and chopped
handful each of **parsley, basil,
   mint** and **tarragon**
2 tablespoons drained **capers**
1 **garlic clove**, crushed
2 tablespoons **olive oil**
4 **swordfish steaks**, about
   150 g (5 oz) each
juice of 1 **lemon**
salt and **pepper**
crisp green salad, to serve

Whisk together the mustard and 250 ml (8 fl oz) of the extra virgin olive oil in a bowl until they have emulsified. Stir in the anchovies.

Chop the herbs and capers together and then add these to the oil mixture along with the crushed garlic. Gradually add more of the extra virgin olive oil until the sauce has a spooning consistency.

Heat a griddle pan until hot. Brush the swordfish steaks on both sides with the olive oil and season well. Griddle the steaks for 2–3 minutes on each side or until cooked through but still very moist.

Add the lemon juice to the salsa verde and serve spooned over the griddled fish with a crisp green salad.

For swordfish with quick salsa verde, cook 4 swordfish steaks, about 150 g (5 oz) each, under a preheated hot grill for 2–3 minutes on each side until cooked through. Meanwhile, place 2 peeled garlic cloves, a small handful of drained capers, a small handful of drained pickled gherkins, 4 drained anchovy fillets in oil, 2 large handfuls of parsley, a handful each of basil leaves and mint, 1 tablespoon Dijon mustard, 3 tablespoons white wine vinegar, 8 tablespoons extra virgin olive oil and some salt and pepper in a food processor or blender. Blend until fully mixed and serve with the swordfish. **Total cooking time 10 minutes.**

creamy spiced lobster tail

Serves **4**

Total cooking time **20 minutes**

2 **egg yolks**, beaten
100 ml (3½ fl oz) **double cream**
30 g (1 oz) **butter**
2 tablespoons **dry sherry**
½ teaspoon **salt**
1 tablespoon **medium curry powder**
4 tablespoons finely chopped **fresh coriander leaves**, plus extra to garnish
450 g (14½ oz) **cooked lobster tail meat**, cut into bite-sized pieces

To serve
lemon wedges
steamed **rice**

Whisk together the egg yolks and double cream in a small bowl until well blended. Melt the butter in a saucepan over a low heat, then stir in the egg mixture and sherry. Cook, stirring, for about 10–12 minutes or until the mixture thickens, but do not allow to boil.

Remove from the heat, then stir in the salt, curry powder and coriander. Stir in the lobster, then return the pan to a low heat and cook gently until heated through.

Spoon into warmed bowls, scatter with chopped coriander and serve with lemon wedges to squeeze over and steamed rice.

For spicy lobster gratin, melt 50 g (2 oz) butter in a saucepan over a low heat, add 2 tablespoons plain flour and 2 tablespoons medium or hot curry powder and cook, stirring, for 1–2 minutes. Gradually whisk in 250 ml (8 fl oz) double cream and 100 ml (3½ fl oz) milk and cook, stirring continuously, for about 5 minutes or until thickened. Cut 500 g (1 lb) cooked lobster tail meat into large pieces and add to the pan. Toss to mix well, season and pour into a shallow casserole dish. Sprinkle over 200 g (7 oz) fresh white breadcrumbs and place in a preheated oven, 220°C (425°F), Gas Mark 7, for 15–20 minutes or until bubbling. Serve warm with a crisp green salad. **Total cooking time 30 minutes.**

red mullet with dill sauce

Serves **4**
Total cooking time **10 minutes**

4 **red mullet fillets**, about
   150 g (5 oz) each
2 tablespoons **olive oil**
5 tablespoons **natural yogurt**
juice of ½ **lemon**
2 **garlic cloves**, crushed
handful of **dill**, finely chopped
salt and **pepper**
grilled **courgettes**, to serve

Season the fish fillets, then rub all over with 1 tablespoon of the oil. Cook skin-side down in a griddle pan over a high heat for 5 minutes. Turn over and cook for a further 3–5 minutes until just cooked through.

Meanwhile, mix together the remaining oil, yogurt, lemon juice, garlic and dill, then season.

Spoon the dill sauce over the fish fillets and serve with grilled courgettes.

For Indian yogurt-baked haddock, mix together 300 ml (½ pint) natural yogurt, 2 tablespoons ground coriander, 2 teaspoons ground cumin, 1 finely chopped green chilli and 1 teaspoon finely chopped fresh root ginger. Place 4 thick haddock fillets, about 175 g (6 oz) each, in an oiled baking dish. Season and pour over the yogurt mixture. Cut 40 g (1½ oz) butter into small pieces and dot over the fish fillets. Cover the dish with foil and place in a preheated oven, 190°C (375°F), Gas Mark 5, for 20 minutes until just cooked through. Transfer the fish to a serving plate. Stir a little more melted butter into the yogurt if it has split, then scatter with chopped fresh coriander and serve. **Total cooking time 30 minutes.**

peppered tuna

Serves **4**
Total cooking time **20 minutes**

5 tablespoons **extra virgin olive oil**

400 g (13 oz) **very fresh tuna steak**

1 tablespoon **black peppercorns**, coarsely crushed

1 tablespoon **balsamic vinegar**

100 g (3½ oz) **rocket leaves**

salt

Parmesan cheese shavings, to serve

Brush 1 tablespoon of the oil over the tuna. Place the crushed peppercorns on a plate, then roll the tuna in the pepper until well coated. Wrap up tightly in a piece of foil. Heat a dry, heavy-based frying pan until smoking hot. Add the wrapped tuna to the pan and cook for 7 minutes, turning every minute or so to cook evenly on each side. Remove from the pan and leave to cool a little.

Whisk the remaining oil with the vinegar until well combined, then season with salt. Just before serving, unwrap the tuna and slice. Toss the rocket with the dressing and arrange on serving plates. Scatter over the tuna and sprinkle with Parmesan shavings to serve.

For slow-cooked tuna with rocket pesto, rub 1 tablespoon olive oil over 4 thick fresh tuna steaks, about 175 g (6 oz) each, place on a baking sheet and season well. Place in a preheated oven, 110°C (225°F), Gas Mark ½, for 25 minutes. Meanwhile, in a food processor or blender, whizz together 100 g (3½ oz) rocket leaves, 2 tablespoons grated Parmesan cheese and a good squeeze of lemon juice. Stir in 5 tablespoons olive oil and 1 teaspoon drained capers and spoon over the tuna to serve. **Total cooking time 30 minutes.**

134

plaice florentine

Serves **4**

Total cooking time **25 minutes**

15 g (½ oz) **butter**, plus extra
  for greasing
1 tablespoon **plain flour**
150 ml (¼ pint) **milk**
50 g (2 oz) **Cheddar cheese**,
  grated
150 g (5 oz) **frozen spinach**
2 large **plaice fillets**, about
  175 g (6 oz) each, halved to
  make 4 thin fillets
25 g (1 oz) **Parmesan
  cheese**, grated
salt and **pepper**
mashed **potato**, to serve

Melt the butter in a saucepan. Stir in the flour and cook for 2 minutes. Slowly whisk in the milk until smooth. Bring to the boil, whisking, then simmer for a few minutes until thickened. Take off the heat, stir in the Cheddar and season.

Place the spinach in a sieve and pour over boiling water until defrosted. Drain well, then roughly chop. Place the fish on a lightly greased baking sheet. Spread a layer of spinach on top of each fillet, then drizzle over some of the white sauce. Sprinkle with the Parmesan.

Bake in a preheated oven, 200°C (400°F), Gas Mark 6, for 10–12 minutes until the fish is just cooked through. Serve immediately with mashed potato.

For plaice with simple parsley sauce, smear a little butter over 4 plaice fillets, about 175 g (6 oz) each. Cook under a preheated hot grill for 7–10 minutes until just cooked through. Meanwhile, mix 4 tablespoons crème fraîche with a large handful of parsley, chopped, and a little milk to loosen. Spoon over the fish and serve alongside some lightly cooked spinach and drained and mashed canned butter beans warmed through in a saucepan. **Total cooking time 10 minutes.**

monkfish with lentils

Serves **4**

Total cooking time **30 minutes**

4 skinless **monkfish fillets**,
  about 150 g (5 oz) each
juice of **1 lemon**
6–8 **basil leaves**, chopped,
  plus extra, torn, to garnish
2 teaspoons **freshly ground
  black pepper**
4 slices of **prosciutto**, halved
  lengthways
4 tablespoons **olive oil**
2 **shallots**, diced
400 g (13 oz) can **green
  lentils**, drained
200 g (7 oz) **baby spinach
  leaves**
2 tablespoons **crème fraîche**
salt

Sprinkle the monkfish with half the lemon juice, the basil and pepper. Wrap each fillet in 2 slices of prosciutto and chill for 10 minutes.

Meanwhile, heat half the olive oil in a frying pan and sauté the shallots for 3–4 minutes. Stir in the lentils and cook for 2–3 minutes to heat through.

Stir the spinach into the lentils, letting it wilt. Squeeze over the remaining lemon juice, stir in the crème fraîche and season with salt.

Heat the remaining olive oil in another frying pan and cook the wrapped monkfish for 6–8 minutes, turning over 2–3 times, until cooked through.

Serve the wrapped monkfish on a bed of lentils and spinach, sprinkled with torn basil leaves.

For monkfish fillets in a smoky tomato sauce,

heat 2 tablespoons olive oil in a frying pan and sauté 2 finely diced shallots for 3–4 minutes. Add 2 crushed garlic cloves, ½ teaspoon smoked paprika and 1 cored, deseeded and thinly sliced red pepper. Pour in a 400 g (13 oz) can chopped tomatoes and simmer for 5–6 minutes. Stir in 100 g (3½ oz) shredded spinach leaves and cook until wilted. Meanwhile, heat 1 tablespoon olive oil in another frying pan and cook 450 g (14½ oz) monkfish fillet, cut into 2.5 cm (1 inch) chunks, for 1–2 minutes on each side. Transfer the monkfish to the tomato sauce and stir in gently. Stir in 2 tablespoons chopped parsley and serve on a bed of cooked green lentils. **Total cooking time 20 minutes.**

grilled sea bass with salsa verde

Serves **4**

Total cooking time **20 minutes**

olive oil, for oiling

4 **sea bass fillets**, about 150 g (5 oz) each

salt and **pepper**

For the salsa verde

3 tablespoons **olive oil**

large handful of **flat leaf parsley**

small handful of **basil**

1 **garlic clove**, crushed

juice of ½ **lemon**

1 tablespoon drained **capers**

To serve

boiled **new potatoes**

green salad

Rub a little olive oil over the fish fillets and season. Heat a griddle pan until smoking hot. Griddle the fish fillets, skin-side down, for 7 minutes until the skin is crisp and golden. Turn over and cook for a further 5 minutes until just cooked through.

Meanwhile, whizz together the salsa verde ingredients in a small food processor or blender until you have a rough paste.

Place the fish on serving plates and spoon over the salsa verde. Serve with boiled new potatoes and a green salad.

For sea bass stuffed with salsa verde, prepare the salsa verde as above. Divide 2 sea bass, about 1.25 kg (2½ lb) each, gutted and scaled, into fillets and season. Thinly slice 1 lemon and lay half the slices down a lightly oiled baking sheet. Cover with 2 fish fillets, skin-side down. Spread the salsa verde all over the fish, then lay the other fillets on top, skin-side up. Cover with the remaining lemon slices. Cook in a preheated oven, 230°C (450°F), Gas Mark 8, for 15–20 minutes until just cooked through. Place on a warmed serving platter and serve with boiled new potatoes and a green salad. **Total cooking time 30 minutes.**

chilli crab

Serves **4**
Total cooking time **25 minutes**

2 tablespoons **vegetable oil**
625 g (1¼ lb) **raw crab claws**
3 **garlic cloves**, crushed
1 tablespoon finely chopped
   fresh root ginger
2–3 **red chillies**, deseeded
   (optional) and finely chopped
200 g (7 oz) can **chopped
   tomatoes**
1 tablespoon **soy sauce**
1 tablespoon **Shaoxing wine**
1 tablespoon **soft dark brown
   sugar**
2 teaspoons **rice vinegar** or
   cider vinegar
2 teaspoons **cornflour**
1 tablespoon **water**
2 **spring onions**, shredded
plain rice, to serve

Heat the oil in a large wok or frying pan. Add the crab claws and cook for about 2 minutes until bright red. Remove from the pan and set aside. Add the garlic and ginger and stir-fry for 30 seconds, then add the chillies followed by the tomatoes, soy sauce, Shaoxing wine, sugar and vinegar. Simmer for 10 minutes, adding a little water if necessary.

Return the crab to the pan and cook for a further 5 minutes until cooked through.

Mix together the cornflour and measurement water until smooth. Stir into the pan and cook for 1 minute to allow the sauce to thicken slightly. Scatter over the spring onions and serve with plain rice.

For sweet & sour chilli crab, heat 2 tablespoons vegetable oil in a large wok or frying pan. Stir-fry 3 crushed garlic cloves and 1 tablespoon finely chopped fresh root ginger for 30 seconds. Add 500 g (1 lb) ready-cooked crab claws, 2 tablespoons each tomato ketchup, sweet chilli sauce and water and a pinch of sugar. Heat through. Squeeze over lime juice to taste and scatter with chopped fresh coriander. **Total cooking time 10 minutes.**

lobster thermidor

Serves **4**
Total cooking time **20 minutes**

15 g (½ oz) **butter**
1 tablespoon **olive oil**
1 **shallot**, finely chopped
3 tablespoons **dry sherry**
1 teaspoon **Dijon mustard**
100 ml (3½ fl oz) **crème fraîche**
2 small **ready-cooked lobsters**, about 625 g (1¼ lb) each
50 g (2 oz) **Gruyère cheese**, grated
salt

Heat the butter and oil in a small saucepan. Add the shallot and cook for 5 minutes until softened. Pour over the sherry and cook for 2 minutes until nearly boiled away. Stir in the mustard and crème fraîche, heat through and season with salt.

Meanwhile, using a large knife, cut the lobsters lengthways in half. Remove the meat from the tail and claws, reserving the main shell halves. Cut the lobster meat into large chunks.

Add the lobster meat to the sauce and warm through. Carefully spoon into the tail cavities of the reserved lobster shell halves and scatter over the Gruyère. Cook under a preheated hot grill for 3–5 minutes until golden and bubbling.

For lobster with thermidor butter, mix together 25 g (1 oz) each softened butter and grated Parmesan cheese, 1 tablespoon crème fraîche, 1 teaspoon Dijon mustard, a squeeze of lemon juice and a pinch of paprika. Use a large knife to cut 2 ready-cooked lobsters, about 625 g (1¼ lb) each, lengthways in half. Remove the meat from the claws and tuck around the tail meat. Dot the thermidor butter all over. Cook under a preheated hot grill for 3–5 minutes until golden and bubbling, then serve. **Total cooking time 15 minutes.**

hot-smoked salmon kedgeree

Serves **4**

Total cooking time **30 minutes**

3 tablespoons boiling **water**
pinch of **saffron threads**
1 tablespoon **vegetable oil**
25 g (1 oz) **butter**
1 **onion**, finely chopped
1 **garlic clove**, finely chopped
1 teaspoon finely grated **fresh root ginger**
1 teaspoon **mild curry powder**
250 g (8 oz) **basmati rice**
750 ml (1½ pints) **fish** or **vegetable stock**
6 **quails' eggs**
300 g (10 oz) **hot-smoked salmon fillets**, skinned
5 tablespoons **crème fraîche**
salt and **pepper**
chopped **flat leaf parsley**, to garnish

Pour the measurement water over the saffron in a jug and leave to infuse. Meanwhile, heat the oil and butter in a large saucepan. Add the onion and gently cook for 5 minutes until softened. Stir in the garlic and ginger and cook for a further 1 minute. Add the curry powder followed by the rice and stir until well coated.

Stir in the stock and saffron with its soaking liquid. Bring to the boil, then leave to simmer for 15 minutes.

Meanwhile, bring a saucepan of water to the boil. Carefully lower in the quails' eggs and cook for 3 minutes. Remove from the pan and cool under cold running water, then shell and halve.

Break the salmon into flakes and add to the rice with the egg halves. Take off the heat, cover and leave to stand for 5 minutes to warm through. Gently stir in the crème fraîche and season. Spoon on to plates and scatter with chopped parsley to serve.

For eggs with smoked salmon dippers, bring a saucepan of water to the boil. Carefully lower in 4 hens' eggs and cook for 4 minutes for a runny yolk. Transfer the eggs to egg cups. Wrap thin strips of smoked salmon around 8 long bread sticks and use to dunk in the eggs. **Total cooking time 10 minutes.**

roast salmon with tartare

Serves **4–6**

Total cooking time **30 minutes**

3 tablespoons **olive oil**
1.5 kg (3 lb) **thick piece of
  salmon**, cut into 2 fillets
1 **lemon**, sliced
handful of **mixed herbs**,
  finely chopped
salt

For the tartare
6 tablespoons **mayonnaise**
2 teaspoons drained **capers**,
  roughly chopped
1 **spring onion**, chopped
1 teaspoon **caster sugar**
1 teaspoon **wholegrain
  mustard**
lemon juice, to taste
handful of **dill**, chopped

To serve (optional)
buttered **new potatoes**
asparagus spears

Brush a large baking sheet with a little of the oil. Place 1 salmon fillet, skin-side down, on the prepared sheet and season with a little salt. Top with the lemon slices and herbs. Season the other salmon fillet and place on top, skin-side up.

Tie pieces of kitchen string around the salmon to secure. Drizzle over the remaining oil. Place in a preheated oven, 220°C (425°F), Gas Mark 7, for 25 minutes or until just cooked through.

Meanwhile, mix together the tartare ingredients and place in a serving bowl.

Serve the fish with the tartare alongside and some buttered new potatoes and asparagus, if liked.

For salmon with preserved lemon, mix together 1 teaspoon each ground cumin, paprika and finely chopped preserved lemon, a handful of fresh coriander, chopped, and 2 tablespoons olive oil. Make slits in the skin of 4 salmon fillets, about 150 g (5 oz) each. Rub the spice mix all over and inside the slits. Set aside to marinate for 5–10 minutes. Heat a griddle pan until smoking hot. Cook the salmon, skin-side down, for 4–5 minutes, then turn over and cook for a further 3 minutes until cooked through. Squeeze over a little lemon juice and serve with some couscous and a tomato salad. **Total cooking time 25 minutes.**

vegetarian

potato, coriander & celeriac soup

Serves **4**

Total cooking time **30 minutes**

1 **onion**, chopped

2 tablespoons **olive oil**

1 **garlic clove**, chopped

½ teaspoon **ground cumin**

½ teaspoon **ground coriander**

pinch of **chilli flakes**

2 small **celeriac**, peeled and finely diced

2 **potatoes**, peeled and finely diced

1 litre (1¾ pints) hot **vegetable stock**

25 g (1 oz) **fresh coriander**, chopped

4 tablespoons **crème fraîche**, to serve

toasted **cumin seeds**, to garnish

Place the onion and olive oil in a pan with the garlic, cumin, ground coriander and chilli flakes. Fry over a medium heat for 1 minute.

Add the celeriac and potatoes, cover with the hot vegetable stock and bring to the boil. Simmer for 15–20 minutes or until the vegetables are tender.

Stir in the fresh coriander and blend with a hand-held blender until fairly smooth.

Serve in warmed bowls with a dollop of crème fraîche, scattered with toasted cumin seeds to garnish.

For spicy potato & celeriac stir-fry, heat 4 tablespoons vegetable oil in a large frying pan or wok and add 1 chopped onion, 1 chopped garlic clove, 1 teaspoon each cumin and crushed coriander seeds and 1 chopped red chilli. Stir-fry over a medium heat for 2–3 minutes. Add 1 large peeled and coarsely grated potato and 1 large peeled and coarsely grated celeriac. Stir-fry over a high heat for 10–12 minutes or until the potato and celeriac are cooked through and tender. Remove from the heat and stir in a large handful of chopped fresh coriander. Season and serve. **Total cooking time 20 minutes.**

squash with stilton fondue

Serves **4**

Total cooking time **30 minutes**

4 **Little Gem** or **other small
    squash**
1 tablespoon **olive oil**
200 g (7 oz) **crème fraîche**
1 tablespoon **cornflour**
200 g (7 oz) **Stilton** or **other
    blue cheese**, rind removed
handful of **thyme leaves**
salt and **pepper**

Cut the squash in half and trim a thin slice off the
rounded back of each half so that they will sit securely,
cut-side up. Scoop out and discard the seeds and fibres,
then score the cut surface of the squash in a criss-cross
pattern. Drizzle over the oil and season to taste. Arrange
on a baking sheet and cook in a preheated oven, 230°C
(450°F), Gas Mark 8, for 15 minutes until tender.

Meanwhile, mix together the crème fraîche and
cornflour, then mash in the cheese with a fork and
add plenty of pepper.

Divide the mixture between the cavities of the squash
halves, scatter over the thyme leaves and return to the
oven for a further 10 minutes until the filling is golden
and bubbling.

For squash & Stilton frittata, heat 4 tablespoons
olive oil in a large, nonstick frying pan. Add 1 sliced red
onion and 1 small butternut squash, peeled, deseeded
and diced, and cook for 5 minutes until softened.
Meanwhile, beat 5 eggs with 2 finely chopped sage
leaves and season well. Reduce the heat to low, then
pour the eggs into the pan. Crumble 50 g (2 oz) Stilton
cheese over the top, then cook very gently for 10–15
minutes until the eggs are just set. **Total cooking time
20 minutes.**

tomato, basil & mozzarella salad

Serves **4**

Total cooking time **20 minutes**

3 tablespoons **extra virgin olive oil**

juice of ½ **lemon**

1 teaspoon **clear honey**

1 teaspoon **mustard**

1 **garlic clove**, crushed

875 g (1¾ lb) **ripe tomatoes**

425 g (14 oz) **mozzarella cheese**, sliced

10–12 **basil leaves**, torn

pepper

Whisk together the olive oil, lemon juice, honey, mustard, garlic and some pepper in a bowl.

Place the tomatoes in a large bowl and pour over boiling water to cover. Leave to stand for 30 seconds, then drain and refresh under cold running water. Peel off the skins and slice the tomatoes.

Layer the tomatoes with the slices of mozzarella and torn basil leaves in individual bowls or one large serving bowl.

Drizzle over the dressing and leave to stand for 5 minutes before serving.

For tomato & mozzarella tart, roll 300 g (10 oz) ready-made chilled puff pastry out on a lightly floured work surface to 25 cm (10 inches) square. Place on a baking sheet and score a 2.5 cm (1 inch) border around the pastry. Bake in a preheated oven, 200°C (400°F), Gas Mark 6, for 10 minutes until golden. Slice 625 g (1¼ lb) ripe tomatoes and 200 g (7 oz) mozzarella cheese and place, slightly overlapping, within the border. Top with 10–12 basil leaves and sprinkle with 2 tablespoons pine nuts. Bake for a further 10–12 minutes until the cheese is melted and the pastry is golden. Meanwhile, whisk together 2 tablespoons olive oil and 1 tablespoon balsamic vinegar and toss with 65 g (2½ oz) rocket leaves. Serve with the baked tart. **Total cooking time 30 minutes.**

roasted chickpeas with spinach

Serves **4**

Total cooking time **20 minutes**

400 g (13 oz) can **chickpeas**, rinsed and drained

3 tablespoons **olive** or **vegetable oil**

1 teaspoon **cumin seeds**

1 teaspoon **paprika**

½ **red onion**, thinly sliced

3 **ripe tomatoes**, roughly chopped

100 g (3½ oz) **young spinach leaves**

100 g (3½ oz) **feta cheese** (optional)

2 tablespoons **lemon juice**

salt and **pepper**

lemon wedges, to garnish

Mix the chickpeas in a bowl with 1 tablespoon of the oil, the cumin seeds and the paprika, and season with salt and pepper. Tip into a large, nonstick roasting tin and roast in a preheated oven, 220°C (425°F), Gas Mark 7, for 12–15 minutes until nutty and golden.

Meanwhile, place the onion and tomatoes in a large bowl with the spinach leaves and toss gently to combine. Heap on to 4 serving plates.

Remove the chickpeas from the oven and scatter over the spinach salad. Crumble the feta over the top, if using, and drizzle each plate with the lemon juice and remaining olive oil. Garnish with lemon wedges and serve immediately.

For chickpea & spinach salad, toss a 400 g (13 oz) can chickpeas, rinsed and drained, with 3 tablespoons olive or vegetable oil and 1 teaspoon each cumin seeds and paprika. Season with salt and pepper. Tip into a large frying pan and heat for 2–3 minutes, stirring occasionally, until hot and fragrant. Remove from the heat, toss with ½ red onion, thinly sliced, and 3 ripe tomatoes, roughly chopped, and fold into 100 g (3½ oz) young spinach leaves, torn. Heap on to serving plates and serve with 100 g (3½ oz) crumbled feta cheese, if liked. **Total cooking time 10 minutes.**

broccoli & blue cheese soufflés

Serves **4**

Total cooking time **30 minutes**

handful of **fine fresh white breadcrumbs**
250 g (8 oz) **broccoli florets**
50 g (2 oz) **butter**, plus extra, melted, for greasing
40 g (1½ oz) **plain flour**
300 ml (½ pint) **milk**
1 teaspoon **smoked paprika**
freshly grated **nutmeg**
4 large **eggs**, separated
100 g (3½ oz) **creamy blue cheese**, crumbled
salt and **pepper**

Brush 4 x 300 ml (½ pint) ramekins with melted butter. Sprinkle with breadcrumbs to coat the base and sides.

Blanch the broccoli in boiling water until almost tender, then pulse in a food processor or blender until smooth.

Melt the butter in a saucepan, add the flour and cook for 2 minutes. Gradually add the milk, stirring continuously, and bring to the boil. Boil for 2 minutes until very thick.

Remove from the heat and stir in the spices and egg yolks. Season well and then stir in the puréed broccoli and cheese.

Whisk the egg whites in a large, grease-free bowl until stiff. Using a metal spoon, carefully fold the egg whites into the broccoli and cheese mixture.

Pour into the ramekins, almost up to the rim. Run your finger around the inside edge of each ramekin to help the soufflés rise straight up. Bake on a hot baking sheet in a preheated oven, 200°C (400°F), Gas Mark 6, for 8–10 minutes or until risen. Serve immediately.

For thick broccoli & blue cheese soup, place a 600 g (1¼ lb) tub ready-made fresh vegetable soup in a saucepan with 400 g (13 oz) finely chopped broccoli florets and bring to the boil. Simmer, uncovered, for 5–6 minutes and then blend with a hand-held blender until fairly smooth. Stir in 200 ml (7 fl oz) double cream and 100 g (3½ oz) crumbled creamy blue cheese. Season and serve in warmed bowls with crusty bread. **Total cooking time 10 minutes.**

wild mushroom tart

Serves **4**
Total cooking time **30 minutes**

375 g (12 oz) **ready-rolled shortcrust pastry**
2 tablespoons **olive oil**
1 **red onion**, sliced
350 g (11½ oz) **mushrooms**, including a variety of **wild** and **chestnut**, trimmed and sliced
2 **eggs**, beaten
100 g (3½ oz) **mascarpone cheese**
1 teaspoon **thyme leaves**
2 teaspoons **wholegrain mustard**
40 g (1½ oz) **Parmesan cheese**, grated
pepper

Use the pastry to line a 23 cm (9 inch) flan tin. Chill while you make the filling.

Heat the olive oil in a frying pan and cook the onion and mushrooms for 5 minutes, stirring frequently.

Meanwhile, beat together the eggs, mascarpone and thyme leaves in a bowl and season with pepper.

Add the onion and mushrooms to the egg mixture and mix well.

Spread the mustard over the flan base. Pour over the filling and level with the back of a spoon.

Sprinkle with the grated Parmesan and bake in a preheated oven, 200°C (400°F), Gas Mark 6, for 20 minutes until golden. Slice into generous pieces and serve hot or cold.

For mushroom & Taleggio bruschetta, heat 2 tablespoons olive oil in a frying pan and sauté 100 g (3½ oz) wild mushrooms, trimmed, with 1 crushed garlic clove for 4–5 minutes. Stir in 1 tablespoon chopped parsley. Toast 8 slices of large baguette on both sides. Top each slice of bread with the mushroom mixture and then a slice of Taleggio cheese. Cook under a preheated hot grill for 1–2 minutes until the cheese is bubbling. Serve warm. **Total cooking time 10 minutes.**

pea & mint risotto

Serves **4**

Total cooking time **30 minutes**

1 tablespoon **olive oil**

2 **shallots**, finely diced

400 g (13 oz) **Arborio risotto rice**

100 ml (3½ fl oz) **white wine**

about 900 ml (1½ pints) hot **vegetable stock**

100 g (3½ oz) **fresh** or **frozen peas**, defrosted

small handful of **mint leaves**, chopped

40 g (1½ oz) **butter**

40 g (1½ oz) **Parmesan cheese**, grated

salt and **pepper**

Heat the oil in a large saucepan and sauté the shallots for 2–3 minutes until softened.

Stir in the rice and cook, stirring, until the edges of the grains look translucent. Pour in the wine and cook for 1–2 minutes until it is absorbed.

Add a ladleful of the hot vegetable stock and cook, stirring continuously, until it has all been absorbed. Repeat with the remaining hot stock, adding a ladleful at a time, until the rice is al dente.

Stir in the peas, mint, butter and half the Parmesan, season with salt and pepper and cook for a further 2–3 minutes.

Serve sprinkled with the remaining grated Parmesan.

For pea & mint pasta salad, cook 200 g (7 oz) fresh penne according to the packet instructions, until al dente, then drain and refresh under cold running water. Meanwhile, cook 350 g (11½ oz) frozen peas in boiling water for 3–4 minutes, then drain and refresh under cold running water. Toss the pasta and peas with 100 g (3½ oz) halved cherry tomatoes, 1 tablespoon chopped mint leaves, 125 g (4 oz) chopped mozzarella cheese and 2 tablespoons pitted black olives in a salad bowl. Add 125 g (4 oz) baby spinach leaves and 3–4 tablespoons Italian salad dressing and toss together gently. **Total cooking time 10 minutes.**

potato & onion pizza

Serves **4**

Total cooking time **30 minutes**

300 g (10 oz) **plain flour**
1 sachet **fast-action dried yeast**
1½ teaspoons **caster sugar**
1 teaspoon **salt**
175 ml (6 fl oz) warm **water**
3 tablespoons **olive oil**, plus extra for oiling
125 ml (4 fl oz) **crème fraîche**
200 g (7 oz) unpeeled **new potatoes**, very thinly sliced on a mandolin
½ **onion**, very thinly sliced on a mandolin
2 teaspoons **dried thyme**
100 g (3½ oz) **Emmental** or **Cheddar cheese**, grated
12 **black olives** (optional)
cracked black pepper

Mix together the flour, yeast, sugar and salt in a large bowl. Make a well in the centre and pour in the measurement water and 2 tablespoons of the oil. Combine to make a soft dough, then roll out to a rectangle about 35 x 25 cm (14 x 10 inches). Transfer to a lightly oiled baking sheet and cook in a preheated oven, 200°C (400°F), Gas Mark 6, for 5 minutes or until just beginning to colour.

Spoon 4 tablespoons of the crème fraîche over the pizza base. Top with the slices of potato and onion, then sprinkle over the thyme and scatter with the cheese. Drizzle the remaining oil over the pizza and return to the oven. Increase the temperature to 220°C (425°F), Gas Mark 7, and bake for about 15 minutes until golden.

Cut the pizza into slices, scatter with the olives, if using, and top with the remaining crème fraîche. Season with cracked black pepper and serve hot.

For creamy potato & onion gnocchi, heat
2 tablespoons olive oil in a frying pan, and cook 1 chopped onion and 2 chopped garlic cloves for 7–8 minutes. Meanwhile, cook 500 g (1 lb) ready-made gnocchi according to the packet instructions, then drain. Add 400 ml (14 fl oz) crème fraîche, 1 teaspoon thyme leaves and 150 g (5 oz) grated Emmental or Cheddar cheese to the onion mixture, and stir for 1 minute. Season generously and stir in the gnocchi. Spoon into 4 bowls and serve immediately, with extra cheese, if liked. **Total cooking time 15 minutes.**

black bean broccoli & mushroom

Serves **4**

Total cooking time **20 minutes**

1 tablespoon **sunflower oil**

1.5 cm (¾ inch) piece of **fresh root ginger**, peeled and sliced into matchsticks

200 g (7 oz) small **broccoli florets**

200 g (7 oz) **shiitake mushrooms**, trimmed

6 **spring onions**, sliced into 1.5 cm (¾ inch) lengths

1 **red pepper**, cored, deseeded and sliced

300 ml (½ pint) **vegetable stock**

500 g (1 lb) **fresh egg noodles**

2 tablespoons **light soy sauce**

1 tablespoon **cornflour**, mixed to a paste with 2 tablespoons water

For the sauce

1 tablespoon **fermented black beans**, rinsed well

1 tablespoon **light soy sauce**

2 **garlic cloves**, crushed

1 **red chilli**, deseeded and chopped

1 tablespoon **Shaoxing wine**

Place all the ingredients for the black bean sauce in a food processor or blender, blend until fairly smooth and set aside.

Heat a wok over a high heat and add the oil. When smoking, add the ginger and stir-fry for a few seconds. Add the broccoli and stir-fry for a further 2–3 minutes.

Add the mushrooms, spring onions and red pepper and stir-fry for 2–3 minutes.

Tip in the black bean sauce and vegetable stock and bring to a simmer. Cook for 2–3 minutes until tender.

Meanwhile, cook the noodles according to the packet instructions, drain and keep warm.

Add the soy sauce, mix in the cornflour paste and cook to thicken for 1 minute. Serve immediately with the egg noodles.

For broccoli, mushroom & black bean stir-fry,

heat 1 tablespoon vegetable oil in a large wok, add 300 g (10 oz) broccoli florets, 300 g (10 oz) trimmed and sliced shiitake mushrooms and 6 sliced spring onions and stir-fry over a high heat for 3–4 minutes. Add a 125 g (4 oz) sachet of ready-made black bean stir-fry sauce and 100 ml (3½ fl oz) water and stir-fry over a high heat for 3–4 minutes. Serve over noodles. **Total cooking time 15 minutes.**

mushroom & herb pancakes

Serves **4**

Total cooking time **30 minutes**

25 g (1 oz) **butter**, plus extra
  for greasing
300 g (10 oz) **baby chestnut
  mushrooms**, trimmed and
  sliced
6 **spring onions**, finely sliced
2 **garlic cloves**, crushed
500 g (1 lb) **tub ready-made
  fresh four-cheese sauce**
300 g (10 oz) **baby spinach
  leaves**
4 tablespoons finely chopped
  parsley
2 tablespoons finely chopped
  tarragon
8 **ready-made savoury
  pancakes**
50 g (2 oz) **Parmesan
  cheese**, grated
salt and **pepper**
lettuce leaves, to serve

Heat the butter in a large, nonstick frying pan, add the mushrooms, spring onions and garlic and stir-fry over a high heat for 6–7 minutes.

Stir in half the cheese sauce and heat until just bubbling. Add the spinach and cook for 1 minute until just wilted. Remove from the heat, stir in the chopped herbs and season.

Take 1 pancake and spoon one-eighth of the filling down the centre. Carefully roll the pancake up and put into a shallow, greased gratin dish. Repeat with the remaining pancakes. Drizzle the remaining cheese sauce over the pancakes, sprinkle with the grated Parmesan and season. Cook under a preheated medium-hot grill for 3–4 minutes until piping hot and turning golden.

Remove from the grill and serve with lettuce leaves.

For creamy mushroom spaghetti, cook 375 g (12 oz) quick-cook spaghetti according to the packet instructions until al dente. Meanwhile, whizz 300 g (10 oz) chestnut mushrooms, trimmed, in a food processor or blender with a 500 g (1 lb) tub ready-made fresh four-cheese sauce, then tip into a large saucepan and bring to the boil. Simmer for 2–3 minutes and then stir in 4 tablespoons chopped tarragon. Drain the pasta, add to the mushroom mixture and mix well, then season and serve straight away. **Total cooking time 10 minutes.**

quinoa & feta with roast veg

Serves **4**

Total cooking time **30 minutes**

1 **red pepper**, cored,
   deseeded and cut into
   chunks
1 **yellow pepper**, cored,
   deseeded and cut into
   chunks
1 **red onion**, cut into wedges
2 **courgettes**, sliced
2 **garlic cloves**, unpeeled
100 g (3½ oz) **butternut
   squash**, peeled, deseeded
   and cut into chunks
2 tablespoons **olive oil**
200 g (7 oz) **quinoa**
200 g (7 oz) **feta cheese**,
   crumbled
small handful of **parsley**,
   roughly chopped
salt and **pepper**

Place the peppers, onion, courgettes, garlic and squash in a roasting tin and toss with the oil. Roast in a preheated oven, 200°C (400°F), Gas Mark 6, for 25 minutes or until tender and browned.

Meanwhile, cook the quinoa in a saucepan of boiling water for 8–9 minutes or according to the packet instructions. Drain and refresh under cold running water, then set aside.

Remove the vegetables from the oven. Squeeze the flesh from the garlic cloves into the vegetables. Season well with salt and pepper.

Stir the quinoa, feta and parsley into the roasted vegetables and serve.

For quinoa, feta & raw vegetable salad, cook 50 g (2 oz) quinoa in a saucepan of boiling water for 8–9 minutes or according to the packet instructions. Meanwhile, in a large bowl, mix together 2 large tomatoes, diced, ½ cucumber, diced, small bunch each of parsley and mint, chopped, 1 small red onion, diced, 50 g (2 oz) shredded mangetout and 1 cored, deseeded and diced red pepper. Drain and refresh the quinoa under cold running water, then stir into the salad ingredients with 2–3 tablespoons ready-made vinaigrette and 100 g (3½ oz) crumbled feta. **Total cooking time 15 minutes.**

haloumi & courgettes with salsa

Serves **4**

Total cooking time **15 minutes**

2 tablespoons **olive oil**

250 g (8 oz) **baby courgettes**, halved lengthways

200 g (7 oz) **haloumi cheese**, thickly sliced

salt and **pepper**

For the salsa

2 **ready-roasted red peppers from a jar**, drained and finely chopped

1 **garlic clove**, crushed

1 **red chilli**, deseeded and finely chopped

finely grated rind and juice of ½ **lemon**

2 tablespoons **extra virgin olive oil**

handful of chopped **mint**

Heat half the olive oil in a large frying pan. Add the courgettes and cook for 2 minutes, then turn over and cook for a further 1 minute until golden. Season to taste, remove from the pan and keep warm.

Add the remaining olive oil to the pan, followed by the haloumi. Cook the cheese for 1–2 minutes on each side until golden.

Meanwhile, mix together all the ingredients for the salsa in a bowl.

Divide the courgettes and haloumi between serving plates and spoon over the salsa to serve.

For roasted haloumi & courgette-stuffed peppers, cut 4 red or yellow peppers in half lengthways, remove the cores and seeds and place on a baking sheet, cut-side up. Drizzle over 1 tablespoon olive oil and season well. Place in a preheated oven, 200°C (400°F), Gas Mark 6, for 10 minutes. Meanwhile, coarsely grate 2 small courgettes and mix with 1 beaten egg and 250 g (8 oz) ricotta cheese. Season and spoon into the peppers. Top the filling with a slice of haloumi and return to the oven for a further 10–15 minutes until golden and just set. **Total cooking time 30 minutes.**

zingy wild mushroom rice

Serves **4**
Total cooking time **30 minutes**

25 g (1 oz) **butter**
1 tablespoon **olive oil**
200 g (7 oz) **wild mushrooms**, trimmed and roughly chopped
1 **onion**, finely chopped
2 **garlic cloves**, crushed
250 g (8 oz) **mixed wild and basmati rice**
750 ml (1¼ pints) **vegetable stock**
finely grated rind and juice of 1 **lemon**
2 **spring onions**, chopped
large handful of chopped **parsley**
½ **red chilli**, chopped
salt and **pepper**

Heat the butter and oil in a large, heavy-based saucepan. Add the mushrooms and cook for 3 minutes until golden, then remove from the pan and set aside. Add the onion to the pan and cook for 5 minutes until softened, then stir in the garlic. Add the rice and stir until coated in the oil, then pour in the stock.

Bring to the boil, then reduce the heat and simmer for about 15 minutes until most of the liquid has been absorbed. Return the mushrooms to the pan, cover and cook very gently for 5 minutes or until the rice is tender. Season to taste and stir in the remaining ingredients before serving.

For mushroom & rice cakes, heat 15 g (½ oz) butter and 1 tablespoon olive oil in a nonstick frying pan. Add 1 crushed garlic clove and 150 g (5 oz) mushrooms, trimmed and finely chopped, and cook for 5 minutes. Remove from the pan and leave to cool for a few minutes. Mix the mushrooms with 1 egg yolk, 300 g (10 oz) ready-cooked rice, 25 g (1 oz) grated Parmesan cheese, the finely grated rind of ½ lemon, a pinch of chilli flakes and a handful of chopped parsley. Season to taste and shape into small cakes with your hands, then lightly coat with plain flour. Heat a little more oil in the frying pan, then cook the cakes for 3 minutes on each side until golden and cooked through. Serve with a tomato salad. **Total cooking time 20 minutes.**

pizza fiorentina

Serves **4**

Total cooking time **15 minutes**

125 g (4 oz) **baby spinach leaves**

4 large **wheat tortillas** or **flatbreads**

150 ml (¼ pint) **ready-made tomato sauce**

125 g (4 oz) **mozzarella cheese**, sliced

4 **eggs**

25 g (1 oz) **Parmesan cheese**, grated

Place the spinach in a sieve and pour over boiling water from the kettle until wilted, then squeeze thoroughly to remove excess water.

Arrange the tortillas or flatbreads on 4 pizza trays. Spoon over the tomato sauce, then scatter over the spinach. Arrange the mozzarella on top, then crack an egg into the centre of each tortilla or flatbread.

Sprinkle the Parmesan over the pizzas, then place in a preheated oven, 220°C (425°F), Gas Mark 7, for 5–7 minutes until the egg whites are just set.

For tomato, spinach & tortilla bake, place 400 g (13 oz) baby spinach leaves in a sieve and pour over boiling water from the kettle until wilted, then squeeze thoroughly to remove excess water. Mix with 250 g (8 oz) ricotta cheese and 75 g (3 oz) crumbled feta cheese. Divide between 8 small tortillas or flatbreads, roll up to enclose the filling and place in a lightly greased ovenproof dish, seam-side down. Pour over 500 ml (17 fl oz) ready-made tomato sauce and sprinkle with 125 g (4 oz) sliced mozzarella cheese and 50 g (2 oz) grated Cheddar cheese. Cook in a preheated oven, 190°C (375°F), Gas Mark 5, for 20 minutes until bubbling and golden. **Total cooking time 30 minutes.**

spicy paneer with peas

Serves **4**

Total cooking time **25 minutes**

2 tablespoons **vegetable oil**
250 g (8 oz) **paneer**, diced
1 **onion**, finely chopped
2 **garlic cloves**, chopped
2 teaspoons finely grated
  fresh root ginger
1 teaspoon **ground coriander**
1 teaspoon **paprika**
1 teaspoon **tomato purée**
125 ml (4 fl oz) hot **vegetable**
  stock
150 g (5 oz) **French beans**
175 g (6 oz) **frozen peas**
150 g (5 oz) **tomatoes**,
  chopped
1 teaspoon **garam masala**
salt and **pepper**
chapattis, to serve

Heat half the oil in a large frying pan. Add the paneer, season well and cook for 3–4 minutes until golden all over. Remove from the pan and set aside. Add the remaining oil to the pan with the onion. Cook for 5 minutes until softened, then add the garlic and ginger and cook for a further 1 minute. Add the spices and cook for 30 seconds.

Stir in the tomato purée and stock and then return the paneer to the pan along with the beans. Season to taste, cover and simmer for 5 minutes. Add the peas and tomatoes and cook for a further 3 minutes, then stir in the garam masala.

Divide between warmed bowls and serve with chapattis.

For spicy paneer & tomato skewers, cut 250 g (8 oz) paneer into large cubes. Mix 1 teaspoon garam masala with ½ teaspoon ground cumin, a pinch of ground turmeric, a handful of chopped fresh coriander and 2 tablespoons vegetable oil. Toss with the paneer, then thread on to metal skewers with some whole cherry tomatoes. Season to taste. Heat a griddle pan until smoking hot, then cook the skewers for 3–5 minutes, turning once, until lightly charred. Serve with green salad and chapattis. **Total cooking time 10 minutes.**

lemon & herb risotto

Serves **4**

Total cooking time **30 minutes**

1 tablespoon **olive oil**

3 **shallots**, finely chopped

2 **garlic cloves**, finely chopped

½ **head of celery**, finely chopped

1 **courgette**, finely diced

1 **carrot**, peeled and finely diced

300 g (10 oz) **Arborio risotto rice**

1.2 litres (2 pints) hot **vegetable stock**

good handful of **mixed herbs**, such as tarragon, parsley, chives, dill

100 g (3½ oz) **butter**

1 tablespoon finely grated **lemon rind**

100 g (3½ oz) **Parmesan cheese**, freshly grated

salt and **pepper**

Heat the oil in a large saucepan, add the shallots, garlic, celery, courgette and carrot and sauté for 4 minutes or until the vegetables have softened. Add the rice and cook, stirring, for 2–3 minutes.

Add a ladleful of the hot stock followed by half the herbs, season well and cook, stirring continuously, until it has all been absorbed. Repeat with the remaining hot stock, adding a ladleful at a time, until the rice is al dente.

Remove from the heat and gently stir in the remaining herbs, the butter, lemon rind and Parmesan. Place the lid on the pan and leave to stand for 2–3 minutes, during which time it will become creamy and oozy. Serve immediately, sprinkled with pepper.

For lemon & vegetable rice, heat 1 tablespoon olive oil in a large frying pan and add 2 chopped shallots, 2 chopped garlic cloves and a 300 g (10 oz) pack stir-fry vegetables and stir-fry briefly. Add 2 x 250 g (8 oz) packs microwaveable rice and the finely grated rind and juice of 1 small lemon. Stir-fry for 5–6 minutes or until piping hot. Serve immediately. **Total cooking time 10 minutes.**

courgette & ricotta bakes

Serves **4**
Total cooking time **30 minutes**

butter, for greasing
2 **courgettes**
100 g (3½ oz) **fresh white breadcrumbs**
250 g (8 oz) **ricotta cheese**
75 g (3 oz) **Parmesan cheese**, grated
2 **eggs**, beaten
1 **garlic clove**, crushed
handful of chopped **basil**
salt and **pepper**

Grease 8 holes of 1–2 large muffin tins. Use a vegetable peeler to make 16 long ribbons of courgette and set aside. Coarsely grate the remainder of the courgettes and squeeze to remove any excess moisture.

Mix the grated courgette with the remaining ingredients and season well. Arrange 2 courgette ribbons in a cross shape in each hole of the muffin tin. Spoon in the filling and fold over the overhanging courgette ends.

Place in a preheated oven, 190°C (375°F), Gas Mark 5, for 15–20 minutes or until golden and cooked through. Turn out on to serving plates.

For mushrooms stuffed with courgettes & ricotta,

brush a little olive oil over 4 large field mushrooms, trimmed, and place on a baking sheet, stem-side up. Grate 1 courgette and squeeze to remove any excess moisture, then mix with 200 g (7 oz) ricotta cheese, 4 drained and chopped sundried tomatoes in oil and 25 g (1 oz) chopped pitted black olives. Season and spoon on to the mushrooms, then sprinkle with 25 g (1 oz) grated Parmesan cheese. Place in a preheated oven, 200°C (400°F), Gas Mark 6, for 15 minutes until golden and cooked through. Serve with ciabatta rolls. **Total cooking time 20 minutes.**

creamy asparagus cappellacci

Serves **4**
Total cooking time **20 minutes**

400 g (13 oz) **cappellacci**
1 bunch of **asparagus spears**,
  trimmed
15 g (½ oz) **butter**
1 **garlic clove**, sliced
150 g (5 oz) **mixed wild**
  mushrooms, trimmed and
  halved if large
75 g (3 oz) **crème fraîche**
salt and **pepper**
Parmesan cheese shavings,
  to serve

Cook the pasta according to the packet instructions until al dente. Add the asparagus 3 minutes before the end of the cooking time and cook until just tender.

Meanwhile, heat the butter in a frying pan, add the garlic and cook for 1 minute, then stir in the mushrooms and cook for 5 minutes until soft and golden. Stir in the crème fraîche.

Drain the pasta and asparagus, reserving a little of the cooking water, and return to the pan. Stir through the mushroom sauce and season, adding a little cooking water to loosen if needed. Spoon into serving bowls and serve scattered with Parmesan shavings.

For asparagus linguine with lemon carbonara sauce, cook 400 g (13 oz) linguine according to the packet instructions until al dente, adding asparagus spears, trimmed, 3 minutes before the end of the cooking time. Meanwhile, mix together 1 egg, 3 tablespoons crème fraîche and a good squeeze of lemon juice in a bowl. Drain the pasta and asparagus and return to the pan. Toss through the egg sauce and serve immediately. **Total cooking time 15 minutes.**

tricolore couscous salad

Serves **4**
Total cooking time **20 minutes**

200 g (7 oz) **couscous**
300 ml (½ pint) hot **vegetable
  stock** or **boiling water**
250 g (8 oz) **cherry tomatoes**,
  halved
2 **avocados**, peeled, stoned
  and chopped
150 g (5 oz) **mozzarella
  cheese**, chopped
handful of **rocket leaves**

For the dressing
2 tablespoons **ready-made
  fresh green pesto**
1 tablespoon **lemon juice**
4 tablespoons **extra virgin
  olive oil**
salt and **pepper**

Mix the couscous and stock or boiling water together in a bowl then cover with a plate and leave for 10 minutes.

Make the dressing. Mix the pesto with the lemon juice and season, then gradually mix in the oil. Pour over the couscous and mix with a fork.

Add the tomatoes, avocados and mozzarella to the couscous, mix well, then lightly stir in the rocket.

For cherry tomato, avocado & mozzarella pasta,
finely chop 300 g (10 oz) cherry tomatoes, 2 peeled and stoned avocados, 50 g (2 oz) rocket leaves and 200 g (7 oz) mozzarella cheese. Place in a bowl with 6 tablespoons ready-made fresh green pesto and 2 tablespoons olive oil. Season and stir to mix well. Leave to stand at room temperature for 15 minutes for the flavours to infuse. Meanwhile, cook 375 g (12 oz) spaghetti according to the packet instructions until al dente. Drain the pasta and transfer to a wide serving dish. Add the cherry tomato mixture, toss to mix well and serve. **Total cooking time 25 minutes.**

gnocchi with spinach & walnuts

Serves **4**

Total cooking time **30 minutes**

1 tablespoon **olive oil**
250 g (8 oz) **baby spinach leaves**
500 g (1 lb) **gnocchi**
200 g (7 oz) **crème fraîche**
½ teaspoon **wholegrain mustard**
75 g (3 oz) **Cheddar cheese**, grated
25 g (1 oz) **Pecorino cheese**, grated
25 g (1 oz) **walnut pieces**

Heat the olive oil in a frying pan and cook the spinach briefly just until it has wilted.

Cook the gnocchi in a saucepan of boiling water according to the packet instructions. Drain.

Place the crème fraîche and mustard in a saucepan, stir in roughly half each of the cheeses and cook for 2–3 minutes, then stir in the spinach and gnocchi to heat through. Stir in the walnuts.

Pour into an ovenproof dish and sprinkle with the remaining cheese. Cook under a preheated hot grill for 3–4 minutes until golden and serve.

For cheesy spinach polenta with creamy mushrooms, heat 2 tablespoons olive oil in a saucepan and sauté 200 g (7 oz) chestnut mushrooms, trimmed and chopped, with 2 chopped shallots and 2 chopped garlic cloves for 5 minutes. Stir in 3 tablespoons crème fraîche with ½ teaspoon wholegrain mustard and 25 g (1 oz) chopped toasted walnuts. Meanwhile, bring 1.5 litres (2½ pints) vegetable stock to the boil in another pan, pour in 275 g (9 oz) instant polenta and cook, stirring continuously, for 5–6 minutes until thick and creamy. Remove from the heat and stir in 100 g (3½ oz) chopped Fontina cheese and 50 g (2 oz) roughly chopped baby spinach leaves. Divide the polenta between 4 warmed bowls, spoon over the creamy mushrooms and serve sprinkled with 2 tablespoons grated Pecorino cheese. **Total cooking time 20 minutes.**

desserts

quick mini lemon meringue pies

Serves **4**
Total cooking time **20 minutes**

4 **ready-made individual
 sweet pastry cases**
12 tablespoons **lemon curd**
1 **egg white**
50 g (2 oz) **caster sugar**

Fill each pastry case with one-quarter of the lemon curd.

Whisk the egg white in a clean, grease-free bowl, until it forms soft peaks and hold its shape. Gradually whisk in the sugar, a little at a time, until the mixture is thick and glossy.

Pipe the meringue mixture in swirls over the lemon curd. Place the pies on a baking sheet and bake on the top shelf of a preheated oven, 200°C (400°F), Gas Mark 6, for 5–6 minutes or until the meringue is just beginning to brown. Cool slightly and serve.

For lemon meringue & blueberry pots, roughly crush 2 ready-made meringue nests and place in the base of 4 dessert bowls. Whip 200 ml (7 fl oz) double cream until it forms soft peaks and then stir in 8 tablespoons lemon curd to create a marbled effect. Spoon over the crushed meringue and top each with 25 g (1 oz) blueberries. **Total cooking time 10 minutes.**

blackberry & apple cranachan

Serves **4**

Total cooking time **20 minutes**

4 teaspoons **porridge oats**
8 teaspoons **caster sugar**
25 g (1 oz) **butter**
1 **dessert apple**, peeled,
 cored and coarsely grated
250 ml (8 fl oz) **vanilla yogurt**
½ teaspoon **ground
 cinnamon**
1 tablespoon **whisky**
400 g (13 oz) **blackberries**,
 plus extra to decorate

Place a small frying pan over a medium-high heat. Add the oats and cook for 1 minute, then add 3 teaspoons of the sugar.

Dry-fry, stirring for 2–3 minutes or until the oats are lightly browned, then tip on to a piece of baking parchment and leave to cool.

Meanwhile, heat a nonstick frying pan over a high heat, add the butter and sauté the apple for 3–4 minutes. When the apple begins to soften, add 4 teaspoons of the remaining sugar and cook until lightly browned. Leave to cool.

Mix together the yogurt, cinnamon, the remaining sugar and the whisky. Stir in the blackberries, crushing them slightly.

Layer the blackberry mixture with the apple in 4 dessert glasses. Top with extra blackberries, sprinkle over the oat mixture and serve.

For warm blackberry & cinnamon compote, heat 625 g (1 ¼ lb) blackberries with 1 teaspoon ground cinnamon, 4 tablespoons caster sugar and a squeeze of lemon juice in a saucepan and bring to the boil. Cook for 5–6 minutes or until the berries have broken down and the mixture has thickened. Serve warm over scoops of ice cream or with vanilla yogurt. **Total cooking time 10 minutes**.

lime cheesecake

Serves **4–6**

Total cooking time **30 minutes**

200 g (7 oz) **digestive biscuits**, crushed
100 g (3½ oz) **butter**, melted
finely grated rind of **1 lime** and 1½ tablespoons juice
300 g (10 oz) **cream cheese**
75 g (3 oz) **icing sugar**, sifted
lime slices, halved, to decorate

Tip the crushed biscuits into a bowl and stir in the melted butter until well coated. Line the sides of a loose-bottomed 20 cm (8 inch) cake tin with clingfilm, then replace the base and press the biscuit mixture evenly over the bottom of the tin. Chill in the refrigerator while making the filling.

Place the lime rind and juice in a clean bowl with the cream cheese and icing sugar, and beat until smooth.

Spoon the filling over the chilled base and smooth down with a palette knife. Decorate with slices of lime. Return to the refrigerator for 20 minutes.

Remove the cheesecake from the tin and gently peel away the clingfilm. Cut into slices and serve.

For lime cheesecake sandwiches, place the finely grated rind of 1 lime and 1½ tablespoons lime juice in a bowl with 300 g (10 oz) cream cheese and 75 g (3 oz) icing sugar, and beat until smooth. Cover and chill the cheesecake filling in the refrigerator for 15 minutes. Divide the mixture between 8 digestive biscuits, then top each one with a second biscuit. Serve immediately. **Total cooking time 25 minutes.**

banoffee layers

Serves **4**

Total cooking time **20 minutes**

6 **digestive biscuits**
2 large **bananas**
50 g (2 oz) **butter**
50 g (2 oz) **soft dark brown sugar**
150 ml (¼ pint) **double cream**
200 ml (7 fl oz) **crème fraîche**
grated **plain dark chocolate**, to decorate

Place the biscuits in a polythene bag and bash with a rolling pin to form fine crumbs. Divide between 4 tall serving glasses and use to line each base.

Mash 1 of the bananas and divide between the 4 glasses, spooning on top of the biscuit crumbs.

Melt the butter in a small saucepan, add the sugar and heat over a medium heat, stirring well, until the sugar has dissolved. Add the cream and cook gently for 1–2 minutes until the mixture is thick. Remove from the heat and leave to cool for 1 minute, then spoon on top of the mashed banana.

Slice the second banana and arrange on top of the caramel, then spoon over the crème fraîche. Decorate with grated plain dark chocolate before serving.

For banoffee & date pudding, lightly whip 300 ml (½ pint) double cream in a large bowl. Crumble in 4 ready-made meringue nests, then fold in 4 sliced bananas and a handful of chopped pitted dates. Swirl over 4 tablespoons ready-made toffee sauce. Spoon into 4 serving dishes, scatter with a handful of pecan nuts and drizzle with a little more toffee sauce. **Total cooking time 10 minutes.**

poached apricots with amaretti

Serves **4**

Total cooking time **30 minutes**

500 g (1 lb) **apricots**, halved
and stoned
4 tablespoons **soft light
brown sugar**
1 **vanilla pod**, split lengthways
5 tablespoons **water**
finely grated rind of 1 **lemon**
200 ml (7 fl oz) **crème fraîche**

For the amaretti
1 **egg white**
75 g (3 oz) **ground almonds**
50 g (2 oz) **caster sugar**

Place the apricots in a heavy-based saucepan with the brown sugar, vanilla pod and measurement water and bring to the boil. Reduce the heat, cover and simmer for 15 minutes until the apricots are tender yet just retaining their shape.

Meanwhile, for the amaretti, whisk the egg white in a grease-free bowl until stiff. Fold in the ground almonds and caster sugar until well mixed. Line a baking sheet with baking parchment and spoon tablespoonfuls of the mixture on to the lined sheet, well spaced apart.

Bake in a preheated oven, 190°C (375°F), Gas Mark 5, for 10 minutes until just beginning to brown. Leave to cool on the paper for 5 minutes, then carefully peel away from the paper and transfer to a wire rack.

Mix the lemon rind into the crème fraîche.

Remove the vanilla pod from the apricots and spoon into serving dishes. Serve with the lemon cream and soft amaretti.

For apricot & peach pavlovas, spoon 2 tablespoons extra-thick double cream into each of 4 ready-made meringue nests. Drain a 400 g (13 oz) can apricots, thinly slice and arrange on top of the cream. Garnish each pavlova with a mint sprig. **Total cooking time 10 minutes.**

strawberry yogurt crunch

Serves **4**

Total cooking time **10 minutes**

4 tablespoons **strawberry jam**
3 tablespoons **soft dark brown sugar**
500 ml (17 fl oz) **Greek yogurt**
8 **digestive biscuits**
1 small **chocolate-covered honeycomb bar**, broken into shards, or extra digestives, crushed, to decorate

Spoon the strawberry jam into the bottoms of 4 tall glasses. Stir the brown sugar into the Greek yogurt and divide half the mixture between the glasses.

Place the biscuits in a polythene bag and bash with a rolling pin to form crumbs, then use the crumbs to cover the yogurt. Spoon over the remaining yogurt and serve sprinkled with shards of chocolate-covered honeycomb or extra crushed digestives.

For marinated strawberry crunch, chop 250 g (8 oz) hulled strawberries and mix with 1 teaspoon lemon juice, 1 tablespoon soft dark brown sugar and the seeds scraped from ½ vanilla pod. Cover and set aside for 15 minutes. Meanwhile, place 8 digestive biscuits in a polythene bag and bash with a rolling pin. Divide the crumbs between 4 glass serving bowls. Top with 500 ml (17 fl oz) Greek yogurt, spoon over the strawberries and serve immediately. **Total cooking time 25 minutes.**

blackberry brûlées

Serves **4**
Total cooking time **10 minutes**

225 g (7½ oz) **blackberries**
2 tablespoons **apple juice**
2–3 teaspoons **caster sugar**,
  to taste
8 tablespoons **Greek yogurt**
2 tablespoons **soft dark
  brown sugar**

Place the blackberries, apple juice and caster sugar in a saucepan and simmer for 2–3 minutes. Spoon into 4 individual ramekins and leave to cool for 2–3 minutes.

Spoon over the Greek yogurt, then sprinkle with the brown sugar.

Cover and chill until required.

For blackberry mousse, place 300 g (10 oz) blackberries, 75 g (3 oz) icing sugar and the juice of ½ lemon in a food processor or blender and blitz to a purée, then pass through a sieve into a large bowl. Stir in 150 ml (¼ pint) double cream and 150 ml (¼ pint) thick natural yogurt and whip until thick. Divide between 4 dishes or glasses, then cover and chill for 10–12 minutes. Serve with dollops of natural yogurt and a few extra blackberries. **Total cooking time 20 minutes.**

mango & custard fools

Serves **4**

Total cooking time **20 minutes**

4 firm, ripe, sweet mangoes
200 ml (7 fl oz) canned
   mango purée
50 g (2 oz) **caster sugar**
150 ml (¼ pint) **double cream**
½ teaspoon crushed
   cardamom seeds, plus extra
   to decorate
200 ml (7 fl oz) **ready-made**
   fresh custard

Stone and peel the mangoes, then cut the flesh into small bite-sized cubes. Place three-quarters of the mango in to a food processor or blender along with the mango purée and sugar and blend until smooth.

Whip the cream with the cardamom seeds until it forms soft peaks and gently fold in the custard. Lightly fold one-quarter of the mango mixture into the custard mixture to give a marbled effect.

Divide half the reserved mango cubes between 4 individual serving glasses and top with half the fool. Layer over two-thirds of the remaining mango mixture and top with the remaining fool.

Decorate with the remaining mango mixture and cubes and a sprinkling of crushed cardamom seeds, then chill until ready to serve.

For mango & cardamom lassi, stone and peel 3 ripe mangoes and place the flesh in a food processor or blender with 4 tablespoons clear honey, 500 ml (17 fl oz) natural yogurt and 1 teaspoon crushed cardamom seeds. Whizz until smooth, pour into 4 tall, ice-filled glasses and serve. **Total cooking time 10 minutes.**

melting chocolate pots

Serves **4**
Total cooking time **25 minutes**

75 g (3 oz) **plain dark chocolate**
100 g (3½ oz) **butter**, plus extra for greasing
75 g (3 oz) **caster sugar**
2 **eggs**
2 tablespoons **cocoa powder**
25 g (1 oz) **plain flour**
icing sugar, for dusting

Grease 4 large ramekins, about 7 cm (3 inches) in diameter. Melt the chocolate and butter in a small saucepan over a very low heat.

Meanwhile, beat the caster sugar and eggs together until pale and creamy.

Pour the melted chocolate mixture into the egg mixture. Beat in the cocoa powder and flour, and continue beating until smooth.

Divide the mixture between the ramekins and cook in a preheated oven, 180°C (350°F), Gas Mark 4, for 10–12 minutes or until they are crisp on top and still melting inside.

Remove from the oven, set aside to cool for 1–2 minutes, then serve dusted with icing sugar.

For vanilla ice cream with melting chocolate sauce, melt 175 g (6 oz) plain dark chocolate, broken into pieces, with 1 tablespoon golden or maple syrup, 15 g (½ oz) butter and 50 ml (2 fl oz) water in a heatproof bowl over a pan of barely simmering water, so that the bowl is not quite touching the surface of the water. Mix until smooth and glossy. Serve drizzled over vanilla ice cream. **Total cooking time 10 minutes.**

blackberry crumble

Serves **4**

Total cooking time **30 minutes**

750 g (1 ½ lb) **blackberries**
2 **oranges**, segmented
finely grated rind and juice of
  1 **orange**
200 g (7 oz) **plain flour**
200 g (7 oz) **butter**, cubed
100 g (3½ oz) **soft light
  brown sugar**
cream, **ice cream** or **custard**,
  to serve (optional)

Mix together the blackberries, orange segments and the orange rind and juice in a bowl.

Place the flour in a separate bowl, add the butter and rub in with your fingertips until the mixture resembles breadcrumbs, then stir in the sugar.

Tip the blackberry mixture into a large pie dish and scatter over the crumble mixture to cover.

Bake in a preheated oven, 220°C (425°F), Gas Mark 7, for 20–25 minutes until golden. Remove from the oven and serve warm with cream, ice cream or custard, if liked.

For blackberry, orange & custard pots, divide 300 ml (½ pint) ready-made fresh custard between 4 dessert glasses. Whizz 200 g (7 oz) blackberries in a food processor or blender with 4 tablespoons caster sugar until smooth and spoon over the custard in the glasses. Peel and segment 2 large oranges, then layer on top of the blackberry purée. Top each glass with a small scoop of vanilla ice cream and serve. **Total cooking time 10 minutes.**

mixed berry eton mess

Serves **4**

Total cooking time **10 minutes**

400 g (13 oz) **mixed berries**,
such as blackberries,
raspberries, blueberries,
plus extra to decorate

400 ml (14 fl oz) **strawberry
yogurt**

300 ml (½ pint) **crème fraîche**

4 tablespoons **icing sugar**,
sifted

4 **meringue nests**, roughly
crushed

Place half the berries in a food processor or blender
and blend until smooth. Transfer to a bowl with the
strawberry yogurt and stir to mix well.

Mix the remaining berries in a bowl with the crème
fraîche and icing sugar. Add to the berry and yogurt
mixture and swirl through to create a marbled effect.

Fold in the crushed meringue and spoon into 4 chilled
dessert glasses.

Serve immediately, decorated with berries.

For summer berry trifles, gently cook 200 g (7 oz)
each raspberries, blueberries and blackberries, 50 g
(2 oz) caster sugar and 2 tablespoons water in a small
saucepan for 2–3 minutes until the fruit is just soft.
Leave to cool. Break 4 trifle sponges into small pieces
and use to line 4 individual dessert bowls or glasses.
Spoon over the berry mixture, followed by 200 ml
(7 fl oz) ready-made fresh vanilla custard. Top each
with a spoonful of crème fraîche, cover and chill until
ready to serve. **Total cooking time 30 minutes.**

lemon–berry vanilla cream tart

Serves **4**

Total cooking time **10 minutes**

200 g (7 oz) **lemon curd**

1 ready-made **sweet pastry tart case**, about 23 cm (9 inches) in diameter

250 g (8 oz) **strawberries**, hulled and sliced

1 **vanilla pod**, split lengthways

200 ml (7 fl oz) **double cream**

1 tablespoon **icing sugar**

Spread the lemon curd over the base of the tart case, then scatter over the sliced strawberries.

Scrape the seeds from the vanilla pod into the cream with the icing sugar and whip until it forms soft peaks. Spoon over the strawberries and serve immediately.

For lemon & vanilla mousse, place 200 ml (7 fl oz) double cream with the seeds scraped from 1 vanilla pod, grated rind of 1 lemon and 50 g (2 oz) caster sugar in a large bowl, and whip until it forms soft peaks. Whisk 2 egg whites in a separate, grease-free bowl until stiff and fold gently into the cream with 3 tablespoons lemon curd. Spoon another 150 g (5 oz) lemon curd into 4 tall serving glasses, then top with the mousse. Cover and chill in the refrigerator for 15–20 minutes or until ready to serve. **Total cooking time 30 minutes.**

quick cherry tiramisu

Serves **4**

Total cooking time **25 minutes**

6 tablespoons **icing sugar**, sifted

100 ml (3½ fl oz) cold **strong black coffee**

12 **sponge fingers**

200 g (7 oz) **mascarpone** or **cream cheese**

150 ml (¼ pint) **double cream**

2 tablespoons **crème de cassis** or syrup from canned cherries

425 g (14 oz) **can black cherries in light syrup**, drained

Stir 2 tablespoons of the icing sugar into the coffee. Arrange the sponge fingers in the bottoms of 4 individual glass dishes, then pour over the black coffee and set aside to soak for about 5 minutes.

Meanwhile, beat the remaining icing sugar into the mascarpone or cream cheese and double cream with the crème de cassis or cherry syrup.

Spoon the cheese mixture over the sponge fingers, cover and chill in the refrigerator for 10–15 minutes. Spoon the drained cherries on top to serve.

For cheat's cherry tiramisu, divide a 400 g (13 oz) can cherry pie filling between 4 individual glass serving dishes. Beat 150 ml (¼ pint) double cream with 300 ml (½ pint) Greek yogurt and 1 tablespoon clear honey until thickened, then crumble 6 sponge fingers into the mixture. Spoon on to the cherries and serve dusted with cocoa powder. **Total cooking time 10 minutes.**

coconut rice with mango & lime

Serves **4**

Total cooking time **30 minutes**

125 g (4 oz) **Arborio risotto rice**

75 g (3 oz) **caster sugar**

300 ml (½ pint) **milk**

400 g (13 oz) can **coconut milk**

½ **mango**, stoned, peeled and cut into small chunks

finely grated rind and juice of 1 **lime**

freshly grated **nutmeg**, to decorate

Place the rice in a heavy-based saucepan with the sugar, milk and coconut milk. Bring to the boil, then reduce the heat and simmer for 20 minutes until the rice has swelled and thickened.

Meanwhile, place the mango in a bowl and mix with the lime rind and juice.

Spoon the cooked rice into serving bowls and place spoonfuls of the mango and lime mixture into the centre of each. Decorate with a little freshly grated nutmeg.

For coconut rice with caramelized banana, place 125 g (4 oz) Arborio risotto rice in a heavy-based saucepan with 75 g (3 oz) caster sugar, 300 ml (½ pint) milk and a 400 g (13 oz) can coconut milk. Bring to the boil, then reduce the heat and simmer for 20 minutes until the rice has swelled and thickened. Meanwhile, cut 4 firm bananas in half lengthways and sprinkle with 4 tablespoons soft light brown sugar and 1 teaspoon ground cinnamon. Heat a nonstick frying pan over a high heat and cook the bananas for 2 minutes on each side or until the sugar has caramelized. Spoon the cooked rice on to serving plates and top with the banana slices. **Total cooking time 25 minutes.**

scone & clotted cream trifles

Serves **4**

Total cooking time **10 minutes**

175 g (6 oz) **strawberries**, hulled and quartered, plus 2 extra, halved, to decorate
4 tablespoons **strawberry jam**
4 tablespoons **clotted cream**
2 **ready-made plain scones**, halved

Place the strawberries in a bowl and mix with the strawberry jam. Divide half the strawberries between the bases of 4 serving glasses and top each with a spoonful of the cream and then a scone half.

Spoon over the remaining strawberries, then decorate each trifle with a strawberry half.

For scone & berry boozy trifle, place 250 g (8 oz) strawberries, hulled, 125 g (4 oz) raspberries and 4 tablespoons strawberry or raspberry conserve in a bowl. Mix well, then transfer to a trifle bowl. Roughly chop 4 ready-made plain scones and scatter over the top, then drizzle with 6 tablespoons dry sherry. Pour over 600 ml (1 pint) chilled ready-made vanilla custard and then spoon over 400 ml (14 fl oz) crème fraîche. Decorate with halved strawberries, if liked. **Total cooking time 15 minutes.**

caramel pear tarte tatin

Serves **4–6**
Total cooking time **30 minutes**

butter, for greasing
2 x 400 g (13 oz) cans **pears
in fruit juice**, drained
5 tablespoons **dulce de leche**
375 g (12 oz) pack **ready-
made sweet shortcrust
pastry**, defrosted if frozen
plain flour, for dusting
ice cream or **cream**, to serve

Line the base of a 23 cm (9 inch) loose-bottomed
cake tin with baking parchment and grease.

Place the pears and dulce de leche in a saucepan
and heat over a gentle heat for 1–2 minutes, stirring
occasionally, until the pears are well coated in the
sauce. Arrange the pears in the base of the prepared
tin in a single layer.

Roll out the pastry on a lightly floured work surface
to a circle slightly larger than the tin and place over
the pears, folding any surplus up the side of the tin.

Place in a preheated oven, 220°C (425°F), Gas Mark
7, for 20 minutes until the pastry is golden and cooked.
Run a knife around the edge of the tart and turn out on
to a serving plate. Serve cut into wedges with ice cream
or cream.

For pan-fried caramelized pears, melt 25 g (1 oz)
butter in a large, heavy-based frying pan. Take 2 x 400 g
(13 oz) cans pears in fruit juice, drain and quarter the
pears and then place in a bowl. Coat the pears in
5 tablespoons dulce de leche and fry in a frying pan
until the sauce is bubbling and the pears are softened.
Serve with scoops of ice cream, drizzled with caramel or
toffee sauce. **Total cooking time 10 minutes.**

berry, honey & yogurt pots

Serves **4**

Total cooking time **10 minutes**

400 g (13 oz) **frozen mixed berries**, defrosted
juice of **1 orange**
6 tablespoons **clear honey**
400 ml (14 fl oz) **vanilla yogurt**
50 g (2 oz) **granola**

Whizz half the berries with the orange juice and honey in a food processor or blender until fairly smooth.

Transfer to a bowl and stir in the remaining berries.

Divide one-third of the berry mixture between 4 dessert glasses or small bowls. Top with half the yogurt.

Layer with half the remaining berry mixture and top with the remaining yogurt.

Top with the remaining berry mixture and sprinkle over the granola just before serving.

For berry & yogurt filo tartlets, cut 2 large sheets of filo pastry in half and cut each half into 4 squares. Brush each square with melted butter. Stack 4 squares on top of each other and repeat with the remaining squares to create 4 stacks. Use to line 4 x 10 cm (4 inch) deep tartlet tins. Bake the filo cases for 8–10 minutes in a preheated oven, 180°C (350°F), Gas Mark 4, until crispy and golden. Leave to cool and remove from the tins. To serve, place 2 tablespoons vanilla yogurt into each tartlet case and spoon over 200 g (7 oz) mixed berries. Dust with icing sugar and serve immediately. **Total cooking time 30 minutes.**

raspberry ripple pain perdu

Serves **4**

Total cooking time **20 minutes**

325 g (11 oz) **frozen raspberries**

1 teaspoon **lemon juice**

2 tablespoons **icing sugar**, plus extra for dusting

2 **eggs**, lightly beaten

125 g (4 oz) **caster sugar**

1 teaspoon **vanilla extract** (optional)

250 ml (8 fl oz) **milk**

4 thick slices of day-old **farmhouse bread** or **brioche**

75 g (3 oz) **butter**

crème fraîche, to serve (optional)

Place the raspberries in a saucepan with the lemon juice and icing sugar, and warm very gently until just beginning to collapse. Blend in a food processor or blender until smooth, then pass through a sieve to remove the seeds.

Whisk together the eggs, caster sugar and the vanilla extract, if using, in a bowl. Add the milk slowly, whisking until smooth and incorporated.

Dip the slices of bread in the egg mixture so that both sides are well coated. Melt the butter in a large, nonstick frying pan and cook the egg-coated bread slices gently for about 2 minutes on each side until crisp and golden.

Remove the bread from the pan and arrange on serving plates. Drizzle with the warm raspberry coulis to create a ripple effect, then dust with icing sugar and serve immediately with crème fraîche, if liked.

For pain perdu with raspberry ripple ice cream,

follow the recipe above to coat 4 thick slices of day-old farmhouse bread or brioche in the egg mixture and fry the bread slices until golden. Remove from the pan and sprinkle both sides of the bread with demerara sugar. Arrange on serving plates and top each slice with a scoop of raspberry ripple ice cream and a dusting of icing sugar. **Total cooking time 10 minutes.**

almost instant peach trifle

Serves **4**

Total cooking time **10 minutes**

175 g (6 oz) **ready-made raspberry Swiss roll**, sliced
400 g (13 oz) can **sliced peaches in juice**, drained, juice reserved
200 g (7 oz) **mascarpone cheese**
200 g (7 oz) **ready-made custard**
2 tablespoons **icing sugar**
150 ml (¼ pint) **double cream**, whipped
25 g (1 oz) **milk** or **plain dark chocolate**, grated, to decorate

Use the Swiss roll slices to line the base of an attractive glass serving dish. Drizzle over 100 ml (3½ fl oz) of the reserved juice, then scatter over the sliced peaches.

Beat the mascarpone with the custard and icing sugar in a bowl, then spoon it over the fruit.

Spoon the whipped cream over the custard, and decorate with the grated chocolate.

For baked peaches with mascarpone, cut 6 ripe but firm peaches or nectarines in half and remove the stones. Place the fruit, cut-side up, in a snug-fitting ovenproof dish. Mix 125 ml (4 fl oz) orange juice with 2 tablespoons clear honey and pour over the fruit. Sprinkle over 2 tablespoons icing sugar and cook in a preheated oven, 180°C (350°F), Gas Mark 4, for 15–18 minutes until tender. Meanwhile, beat 2 extra tablespoons icing sugar into 200 g (7 oz) mascarpone cheese, then cover and chill until required. Remove the fruit from the oven and arrange in serving dishes. Scatter over 100 g (3½ oz) raspberries, if liked, and serve with the sweetened mascarpone. **Total cooking time 30 minutes.**

almond affogato

Serves **4**

Total cooking time **10 minutes**

4 scoops of **nougat** or **vanilla ice cream**

4 drops of **almond extract**

4 shots of **hot strong coffee**

1 tablespoon **flaked almonds**, toasted

almond biscuits, to serve (optional)

Place a scoop of ice cream in each of 4 heatproof serving glasses.

Stir the almond extract into the hot coffee, then pour 1 shot over each scoop of ice cream.

Scatter with the toasted almonds and serve with almond biscuits, if liked.

For affogato-style tiramisu, stir 4 drops of almond extract into 125 ml (4 fl oz) cold strong coffee. Arrange 16 sponge fingers in a dish, then pour over the coffee and set aside for 5 minutes to soak. Break up the sponge fingers and divide half of them between 4 tall freezer-proof glasses. Spoon a small scoop of nougat or vanilla ice cream into each of the glasses, and top with the remaining sponge fingers. Top with another small scoop of ice cream, then place in the freezer for 10–15 minutes until firm. Sprinkle with a dusting of cocoa powder and 1 tablespoon toasted flaked almonds and serve with almond biscuits or rolled ice-cream wafers, if liked. **Total cooking time 30 minutes.**

index

affogato-style tiramisu 232

almonds
affogato-style tiramisu 232
almond affogato 232
poached apricots with amaretti 202

almost instant peach trifle 230

anchovies
broad bean & anchovy salad 40
Caesar salad 48
open chicken Caesar sandwich 48
roasted peppers with tomatoes & anchovies 40
swordfish with quick salsa verde 128
swordfish with salsa verde 128

apples
blackberry & apple cranachan 196
blue cheese soufflé 42
blue cheese Waldorf salad 42

apricots
apricot & peach pavlovas 202
gammon steaks with apricot sauce 96
poached apricots with amaretti 202
spiced apricot-glazed gammon 96

artichoke hearts
chicken, prawn & chorizo pilaf 72
quick paella 72
Tuscan tart with artichokes & lemon 64

Asian-style teriyaki beef on lettuce platters 54

asparagus
asparagus linguine with lemon carbonara sauce 186
asparagus mimosa 30
asparagus tart 30

creamy asparagus cappellacci 186

aubergines
baked lamb-stuffed aubergines 76

avocados
cherry tomato, avocado & mozzarella pasta 188
prawn & avocado tostada 108

bacon
creamy scallops with leeks 126
liver & bacon tagliatelle 80
scallop & bacon kebabs with leeks 126
warm tomato, liver and bacon salad 80

bananas
banoffee & date pudding 200
banoffee layers 200
coconut rice with caramelized bananas 220

basil
tomato, basil & mozzarella salad 156

beans
beef carpaccio & bean salad 56
broad beans & anchovy salad 40
clams in black bean sauce 124
prawn & black bean chilli 108

beef
Asian-style teriyaki beef on lettuce platters 54
beef & peppercorn stroganoff 86
beef carpaccio & bean salad 56
beef skewers with satay sauce 54
cheat's spiced beef & mushroom pie 86
green peppercorn burgers with blue cheese sauce 82
harissa beef burgers 92
harissa beef fajitas 92
quick beef carpaccio & bean salad 56

steak with peppercorn sauce 82

beetroot
hot potato blinis with beetroot 16

berries
berry & yogurt filo tartlets 226
berry, honey & yogurt pots 226
mixed berry Eton mess 214
summer berry trifles 214

black bean broccoli & mushroom 168

black bean sauce
broccoli, mushroom & black bean stir-fry 168
mussels in black bean sauce 124

blackberries
blackberry & apple cranachan 196
blackberry brûlées 206
blackberry crumble 212
blackberry mousse 206
blackberry, orange & custard pots 212
warm blackberry & cinnamon compote 196

bloody Mary gazpacho 12

blueberries
lemon meringue & blueberry pots 194

bread
Brie & thyme melts 50
Caesar salad 48
cheese & onion bruschetta 46
eggs with smoked salmon dippers 148
mushroom & Taleggio bruschetta 162
open chicken Caesar sandwich 48
pain perdu with raspberry ripple ice cream 228
raspberry ripple pain perdu 228

bream
salt-baked bream 118
sea bream baked on salt 118

broccoli
black bean broccoli & mushroom 168

broccoli & blue cheese soufflés 160
broccoli, mushroom & black bean stir-fry 168
thick broccoli & blue cheese soup 160

butternut squash
quinoa & feta with roast veg 172
squash & Stilton frittata 154

Caesar salad 48

caramel pear tarte tatin 224

celeriac
celeriac remoulade & ham rolls 26
celeriac remoulade with ham 26
potato, coriander & celeriac soup 152
spicy potato & celeriac stir-fry 152

cheese
asparagus tart 30
baked figs wrapped in prosciutto 20
baked lamb-stuffed aubergines 76
baked mushrooms with Taleggio 24
baked peaches with mascarpone 230
blue cheese soufflé 42
blue cheese Waldorf salad 42
Brie & thyme melts 50
broccoli & blue cheese soufflés 160
cheese & onion bruschetta 46
cheese-stuffed onions 46
cheesy spinach polenta with creamy mushrooms 190
cherry tomato, avocado & mozzarella pasta 188
courgette & ricotta bakes 184
creamy asparagus cappellacci 186
fig & ham country salad 20
gnocchi with spinach & walnuts 190
gorgonzola with warm Marsala pears 44

green peppercorn burgers with blue cheese sauce 82
haloumi & courgette-stuffed peppers 174
haloumi & courgettes with salsa 174
lamb & olive stew 94
lemon & herb risotto 182
lime cheesecake 198
lime cheesecake sandwiches 198
lobster thermidor 144
mushroom & herb pancakes 170
mushroom & rice cakes 176
mushroom & Taleggio bruschetta 162
mushrooms stuffed with courgettes & ricotta 184
pear, walnut & gorgonzola salad 44
peppered tuna 134
pizza fiorentina 178
plaice Florentine 136
polenta-crusted pork 74
potato & onion pizza 166
prawns with sundried tomato feta dip 28
quick cherry tiramisu 218
quinoa & feta with roast veg 172
quinoa, feta & raw vegetable salad 172
roasted chickpeas with spinach 158
slow-cooked tuna with rocket pesto 134
spicy paneer & tomato skewers 180
spicy paneer with peas 180
squash & Stilton frittata 154
squash with Stilton fondue 154
stuffed mussels 104
thick broccoli & blue cheese soup 160
tomato & mozzarella tart 156
tomato, basil & mozzarella salad 156
tomato, prawn & feta salad 28

tomato, spinach & tortilla bake 178
tricolore couscous salad 188
whole baked cheese with garlic & thyme 50
wild mushroom tart 162
cherries
cheat's cherry tiramisu 218
quick cherry tiramisu 218
chicken
butter & lemon roasted chicken 70
chicken, prawn & chorizo pilaf 72
chicken satay 62
chicken satay skewers 62
hoisin chicken pancakes 58
open chicken Caesar sandwich 48
pan-fried thighs with lemon & butter 70
quick paella 72
Tuscan tart with artichokes & lemon 64
Tuscan-style tarts 64
chicken livers
liver & bacon tagliatelle 80
warm tomato, liver and bacon salad 80
chickpeas
chickpea & spinach salad 158
roasted chickpeas with spinach 158
chillies
chilli & garlic-braised clams 116
chilli crab 142
chilli spaghetti vongole 116
prawn & black bean chilli 108
salt & pepper squid bites with chilli jam 34
sweet & sour chilli crab 142
Chinese duck noodles 68
chocolate
almost instant peach trifle 230
banoffee layers 200
melting chocolate pots 210

vanilla ice cream with melting chocolate sauce 210
chorizo
chicken, prawn & chorizo pilaf 72
creamy gnocchi & chorizo bake 98
panfried gnocchi & chorizo salad 98
quick paella 72
clams
chilli & garlic-braised clams 116
chilli spaghetti vongole 116
clam & tomato linguine 110
clams in black bean sauce 124
Manhattan clam chowder 110
clementines
smoked duck citrus salad 60
warm duck, clementine & walnut salad 60
coconut milk
coconut rice with caramelized bananas 220
coconut rice with mango & lime 220
coffee
affogato-style tiramisu 232
almond affogato 232
quick cherry tiramisu 218
courgettes
courgette & ricotta bakes 184
haloumi & courgette-stuffed peppers 174
haloumi & courgettes with salsa 174
mushrooms stuffed with courgettes & ricotta 184
red mullet with dill sauce 132
couscous
griddled lamb with pine nuts 76
salmon with preserved lemon 148
spiced apricot-glazed gammon 96

tricolore couscous salad 188
crab
chilli crab 142
crab & mango salad 36
sweet & sour chilli crab 142
Vietnamese spring rolls 22
wild rice, crab & mango salad 36
crayfish cocktail 18
custard
almost instant peach trifle 230
blackberry, orange & custard pots 212
mango & custard fools 208
scone & berry boozy trifle 222
summer berry trifles 214

dates
banoffee & date pudding 200
strawberry yogurt crunch 204
duck
Chinese duck noodles 68
smoked duck citrus salad 60
stir-fried duck with orange rice 68
warm duck, clementine & walnut salad 60

easy spiced lamb pilaf 100
eggs
asparagus mimosa 30
broccoli & blue cheese soufflés 160
Caesar salad 48
courgette & ricotta bakes 184
creamy spiced lobster tail 130
eggs with smoked salmon dippers 146
hot-smoked salmon kedgeree 146
mushroom & rice cakes 176
pizza fiorentina 178
squash & Stilton frittata 154
wild mushroom tart 162

fennel
sea bream baked on salt 118

figs
baked figs wrapped in prosciutto 20
fig & ham country salad 20

gammon
gammon steaks with apricot sauce 96
spiced apricot-glazed gammon 96

ginger
baked turkey breast with ginger & coriander 66
ginger & coriander turkey burgers 66
sesame tuna with ginger dressing 112
tuna carpaccio with ginger salad 112

gnocchi
creamy gnocchi & chorizo bake 98
creamy potato & onion gnocchi 166
gnocchi with spinach & walnuts 190
pan-fried gnocchi & chorizo salad 98

grapefruit
halibut ceviche with grapefruit 106
spicy halibut & grapefruit salad 106

halibut
halibut ceviche with grapefruit 106
spicy halibut & grapefruit salad 106

haloumi & courgette-stuffed peppers 174
haloumi & courgettes with salsa 174

ham
baked figs wrapped in prosciutto 20
celeriac remoulade & ham rolls 26
celeriac remoulade with ham 26
fig & ham country salad 20

ice cream
affogato-style tiramisu 232
almond affogato 232
pain perdu with raspberry ripple ice cream 228
vanilla ice cream with melting chocolate sauce 210

Indian yogurt-baked haddock 132

lamb
baked lamb-stuffed aubergines 76
easy spiced lamb pilaf 100
griddled lamb with pine nuts 76
grilled tandoori lamb chops 84
lamb & olive stew 94
lamb cutlets with fried polenta 94
lamb cutlets with pea mash 88
lamb racks with rosemary & garlic 88
rack of lamb with harissa 100
tandoori roast rack of lamb 84

leeks
creamy scallops with leeks 126
scallop & bacon kebabs with leeks 126

lemon curd
lemon & vanilla mousse 216
lemon meringue & blueberry pots 194
lemon-berry vanilla cream tart 216
quick mini lemon meringue pies 194

lemons
asparagus linguine with lemon carbonara sauce 186
butter & lemon roasted chicken 70
lemon & herb risotto 182
lemon & vanilla mousse 216
lemon & vegetable rice 182

pan-fried thighs with lemon & butter 70
salmon with preserved lemon 148
Tuscan tart with artichokes & lemon 64

lentils
monkfish with lentils 138

lettuce
Asian-style teriyaki beef on lettuce platters 54
Caesar salad 48

limes
coconut rice with mango & lime 220
grilled pork with plum salsa 78
halibut ceviche with grapefruit 106
lime cheesecake 198
lime cheesecake sandwiches 198

lobster
creamy spiced lobster tail 130
lobster thermidor 144
lobster with thermidor butter 144
spicy lobster gratin 130

mackerel
mackerel with roasted tomatoes 120
mackerel and sunblush tomato salad 120

mangoes
coconut rice with mango & lime 220
crab & mango salad 36
mango & cardamom lassi 208
mango & custard fools 208
wild rice, crab & mango salad 36

meringue nests
apricot & peach pavlovas 202
banoffee & date pudding 200
lemon meringue & blueberry pots 194
mixed berry Eton mess 214

Mexican-style seafood cocktail 18

mint
pea & mint pasta salad 164
pea & mint risotto 164
swordfish with salsa verde 128

monkfish
monkfish fillets in a smoky tomato sauce 138
monkfish with lentils 138

moules marinières 38

mushrooms
baked mushrooms with Taleggio 24
beef & peppercorn stroganoff 86
black bean broccoli & mushroom 168
broccoli, mushroom & black bean stir-fry 168
cheat's spiced beef & mushroom pie 86
cheesy spinach polenta with creamy mushrooms 190
chunky mushroom and tarragon soup 32
creamy mushroom spaghetti 170
creamy veal escalopes 90
mushroom & herb pancakes 170
mushroom & rice cakes 176
mushroom & Taleggio bruschetta 162
mushrooms stuffed with courgettes & ricotta 184
tarragon mushroom toasts 32
wild mushroom tart 162
zingy wild mushroom rice 176

mussels
crispy baked mussels 36
moules marinières 38
mussels in black bean sauce 124
smoked mussel bruschetta 104
stuffed mussels 104

noodles
broccoli, mushroom & black bean stir-fry 168

Chinese duck noodles 68
Vietnamese spring rolls 22
Vietnamese summer rolls 22

oats
blackberry & apple cranachan 196
olives
lamb & olive stew 94
onions
cheese & onion bruschetta 46
cheese-stuffed onions 46
creamy potato & onion gnocchi 166
potato & onion pizza 166
oranges
blackberry, orange & custard pots 212
sesame tuna with ginger dressing 112
stir-fried duck with orange rice 68

paella
quick paella 72
paneer
spicy paneer & tomato skewers 180
spicy paneer with peas 180
pasta
asparagus linguine with lemon carbonara sauce 186
cherry tomato, avocado & mozzarella pasta 188
chilli spaghetti vongole 116
corn and salmon pasta 14
creamy asparagus cappellacci 186
creamy mushroom spaghetti 170
liver & bacon tagliatelle 80
pea & mint pasta salad 164
pastry
berry & yogurt filo tartlets 226
caramel pear tarte tatin 224
lemon-berry vanilla cream tart 216

quick mini lemon meringue pies 194
tomato & mozzarella tart 156
Tuscan-style tarts 64
wild mushroom tart 162
peaches
almost instant peach trifle 230
apricot & peach pavlovas 202
baked peaches with mascarpone 230
pears
caramel pear tarte tatin 224
gorgonzola with warm Marsala pears 44
panfried caramelized pears 224
pear, walnut & gorgonzola salad 44
pork steaks with pears 74
peas
chicken, prawn & chorizo pilaf 72
lamb cutlets with pea mash 88
pea & mint pasta salad 164
pea & mint risotto 164
spicy paneer with peas 180
peppers
black bean broccoli & mushroom 168
haloumi & courgette-stuffed peppers 174
haloumi & courgettes with salsa 174
monkfish fillets in a smoky tomato sauce 138
quinoa & feta with roast veg 172
quinoa, feta & raw vegetable salad 172
roasted peppers with tomatoes & anchovies 40
roasted tomato gazpacho 12
Tuscan-style tarts 64
veal salad 90
pizza
pizza fiorentina 178
potato & onion pizza 166

plaice
plaice Florentine 136
plaice with simple parsley sauce 136
plums
grilled pork with plum salsa 78
pork chops with plum relish 78
poached apricots with amaretti 202
polenta
cheesy spinach polenta with creamy mushrooms 190
lamb & olive stew 94
lamb cutlets with fried polenta 94
polenta-crusted pork 74
pork
grilled pork with plum salsa 78
polenta-crusted pork 74
pork chops with plum relish 78
pork steaks with pears 74
Vietnamese spring rolls 22
potatoes
apricot-glazed gammon steaks 96
cheat's spiced beef & mushroom pie 86
creamy potato & onion gnocchi 166
hot potato blinis with beetroot 16
lamb cutlets with pea mash 88
potato & chive soup 16
potato & onion pizza 166
spicy potato & celeriac stir-fry 152
prawns
chicken, prawn & chorizo pilaf 72
Mexican-style seafood cocktail 18
prawn & avocado tostada 108
prawn & black bean chilli 108
prawns with sundried tomato feta dip 28
quick paella 72
tomato, prawn & feta salad 28

Vietnamese spring rolls 22
Vietnamese summer rolls 22

quinoa
quinoa & feta with roast veg 172
quinoa, feta & raw vegetable salad 172

rack of lamb with harissa 100
radishes
crab & mango salad 36
tuna carpaccio with ginger salad 112
raspberries
pain perdu with raspberry ripple ice cream 228
raspberry ripple pain perdu 228
scone & berry boozy trifle 222
red mullet with dill sauce 132
rice
beef & peppercorn stroganoff 86
chicken, prawn & chorizo pilaf 72
chicken satay 62
coconut rice with caramelized bananas 220
coconut rice with mango & lime 220
creamy scallops with leeks 126
easy spiced lamb pilaf 100
hot-smoked salmon kedgeree 146
lemon & herb risotto 182
lemon & vegetable rice 182
mushroom & rice cakes 176
pea & mint risotto 164
quick paella 72
seafood risotto 114
stir-fried duck with orange rice 68
wild rice, crab & mango salad 36
zingy wild mushroom rice 176

rice paper wrappers
    Vietnamese summer rolls
      22
rocket
    cherry tomato, avocado
      & mozzarella pasta
      188
    mackerel with roasted
      tomatoes 120
    peppered tuna 134
    polenta-crusted pork 74
    slow-cooked tuna with
      rocket pesto 134
    tomato & mozzarella tart
      156
    tricolore couscous salad
      188
    tuna carpaccio with ginger
      salad 112
    veal salad 90
rosemary
    lamb cutlets with pea mash
      88
    lamb racks with rosemary
      & garlic 88

saffron
    hot-smoked salmon
      kedgeree 146
    quick paella 72
sage
    squash & Stilton frittata
      154
salads
    blue cheese Waldorf salad
      42
    Caesar salad 48
    chickpea & spinach salad
      158
    crab & mango salad 36
    fig & ham country salad
      20
    mackerel and sunblush
      tomato salad 120
    pan-fried gnocchi &
      chorizo salad 98
    pea & mint pasta salad
      164
    pear, walnut & gorgonzola
      salad 44
    quinoa, feta & raw
      vegetable salad 172
    spicy halibut & grapefruit
      salad 106
    tomato, basil & mozzarella
      salad 156

tomato, prawn & feta salad
    28
tricolore couscous salad
    188
tuna carpaccio with ginger
    salad 112
veal salad 90
warm tomato, liver and
    bacon salad 80
salmon
    honey mustard salmon
      122
    roast salmon with tartare
      148
    salmon with mustard
      Hollandaise 122
    salmon with preserved
      lemon 148
salt
    salt & pepper squid bites
      34
    salt & pepper squid bites
      with chilli jam 34
    salt-baked bream 118
    sea bream baked on salt
      118
scallops
    creamy scallops with leeks
      126
    Mexican-style seafood
      cocktail 18
    scallop & bacon kebabs
      with leeks 126
scones
    scone & berry boozy trifle
      222
    scone and clotted cream
      trifles 222
sea bass
    grilled sea bass with salsa
      verde 140
    sea bass stuffed with salsa
      verde 140
seafood
    mixed seafood casserole
      114
    seafood risotto 114
sesame seeds
    sesame tuna with ginger
      dressing 112
smoked duck citrus salad 60
smoked mussel bruschetta
    104
smoked salmon
    corn cakes with smoked
      salmon 14

corn and salmon pasta 14
eggs with smoked salmon
    dippers 148
hot-smoked salmon
    kedgeree 146
soups
    chunky mushroom and
      tarragon soup 32
    potato, coriander &
      celeriac soup 152
    thick broccoli & blue
      cheese soup 160
spinach
    cheese-stuffed onions 46
    cheesy spinach polenta
      with creamy mushrooms
      190
    chickpea & spinach salad
      158
    creamy veal escalopes 90
    easy spiced lamb pilaf
      100
    gnocchi with spinach &
      walnuts 190
    monkfish fillets in a smoky
      tomato sauce 138
    monkfish with lentils 138
    mushroom & herb
      pancakes 170
    pea & mint pasta salad
      164
    pizza fiorentina 178
    plaice Florentine 136
    plaice with simple parsley
      sauce 136
    roasted chickpeas with
      spinach 158
    tomato, spinach & tortilla
      bake 178
sponge fingers
    affogato-style tiramisu
      232
    cheat's cherry tiramisu
      218
spring onions
    broccoli, mushroom &
      black bean stir-fry 168
    Chinese duck noodles 68
    clams in black bean sauce
      124
    hoisin chicken pancakes
      58
    mushroom & herb
      pancakes 170
    sesame tuna with ginger
      dressing 112

stir-fried duck with orange
    rice 68
zingy wild mushroom rice
    176
spring rolls
    Vietnamese spring rolls 22
squash
    quinoa & feta with roast
      veg 172
    squash & Stilton frittata
      154
    squash with Stilton fondue
      154
squid
    salt & pepper squid bites
      34
    salt & pepper squid bites
      with chilli jam 34
    steak with peppercorn
      sauce 82
strawberries
    lemon-berry vanilla cream
      tart 216
    marinated strawberry
      crunch 204
    scone & berry boozy trifle
      222
    scone and clotted cream
      trifles 222
    strawberry yogurt crunch
      204
sugar snap peas
    Chinese duck noodles 68
    stir-fried duck with orange
      rice 68
summer berry trifles 214
sweet & sour chilli crab 142
sweetcorn
    corn cakes with smoked
      salmon 14
    corn and salmon pasta 14
swordfish
    swordfish with quick salsa
      verde 128
    swordfish with salsa verde
      128

tandoori roast rack of
    lamb 84
tarragon
    chunky mushroom and
      tarragon soup 32
    creamy mushroom
      spaghetti 170
    mushroom & herb
      pancakes 170

stuffed mussels 104
swordfish with salsa verde 128
tarragon mushroom toasts 32
tarts
Tuscan tart with artichokes & lemon 64
Thai red curry paste
chicken satay 62
chicken satay skewers 62
thick broccoli & blue cheese soup 160
thyme
Brie & thyme melts 50
sea bream baked on salt 118
squash with Stilton fondue 154
Tuscan-style tarts 64
whole baked cheese with garlic & thyme 50
tomatoes
bloody Mary gazpacho 12
broad beans & anchovy salad 40
cherry tomato, avocado & mozzarella pasta 188
chickpea & spinach salad 158
chilli & garlic-braised clams 116
chilli crab 142
clam & tomato linguine 110
creamy gnocchi & chorizo bake 98
halibut ceviche with grapefruit 106
harissa beef burgers 92
mackerel with roasted tomatoes 120
mackerel and sunblush tomato salad 120
mixed seafood casserole 114
monkfish fillets in a smoky tomato sauce 138
mushrooms stuffed with courgettes & ricotta 184
pan-fried gnocchi & chorizo salad 98
pea & mint pasta salad 164

quinoa, feta & raw vegetable salad 172
roasted chickpeas with spinach 158
roasted peppers with tomatoes & anchovies 40
roasted tomato gazpacho 12
salt & pepper squid bites with chilli jam 34
smoked mussel bruschetta 104
spicy paneer & tomato skewers 180
spicy paneer with peas 180
tomato & mozzarella tart 156
tomato, basil & mozzarella salad 156
tomato, prawn & feta salad 28
tomato, spinach & tortilla bake 178
tricolore couscous salad 188
Tuscan-style tarts 64
veal salad 90
warm tomato, liver and bacon salad 80
tortillas
harissa beef fajitas 92
pizza fiorentina 178
prawn & avocado tostada 108
prawn & black bean chilli 108
tomato, spinach & tortilla bake 178
tricolore couscous salad 188
tuna
peppered tuna 134
sesame tuna with ginger dressing 112
slow-cooked tuna with rocket pesto 134
tuna carpaccio with ginger salad 112
turkey
baked turkey breast with ginger & coriander 66
ginger & coriander turkey burgers 66
Tuscan tart with artichokes & lemon 64

Tuscan-style tarts 64

vanilla
lemon & vanilla mousse 216
lemon-berry vanilla cream tart 216
poached apricots with amaretti 202
vanilla ice cream with melting chocolate sauce 210
veal
creamy veal escalopes 90
veal salad 90
vegetables
lemon & vegetable rice 182
Vietnamese spring rolls 22
Vietnamese summer rolls 22

walnuts
blue cheese Waldorf salad 42
cheesy spinach polenta with creamy mushrooms 190
gnocchi with spinach & walnuts 190
pear, walnut & gorgonzola salad 44
polenta-crusted pork 74
smoked duck citrus salad 60
stuffed mussels 104
veal salad 90
warm duck, clementine & walnut salad 60
warm blackberry & cinnamon compote 196
warm tomato, liver and bacon salad 80
watercress
crab & mango salad 36
smoked duck citrus salad 60
whisky
blackberry & apple cranachan 196
wild rice
wild rice, crab & mango salad 36
zingy wild mushroom rice 176

yogurt
berry & yogurt filo tartlets 226
berry, honey & yogurt pots 226
blackberry & apple cranachan 196
blackberry brûlées 206
blackberry mousse 206
cheat's cherry tiramisu 218
grilled tandoori lamb chops 84
Indian yogurt-baked haddock 132
mango & cardamom lassi 208
mixed berry Eton mess 214
rack of lamb with harissa 100
red mullet with dill sauce 132
strawberry yogurt crunch 204
tandoori roast rack of lamb 84

zingy wild mushroom rice 176

acknowledgements

Commissioning editor: Eleanor Maxfield
Editor: Polly Poulter
Designer: Tracy Killick
Production controller: Allison Gonsalves
Indexer: Isobel McLean

Photography: Octopus Publishing Group Stephen Conroy 55, 69, 97, 127, 201, 203, 221, 223, 225; Will Heap 1, 2-3, 4-5, 6 left, 7, 8 left, 13, 17, 21, 25, 27, 31, 33, 37, 43, 49, 61, 79, 85, 87, 101, 111, 113, 117, 119, 131, 153, 161, 169, 171, 183, 189, 192-193, 195, 197, 209, 213, 215, 227; Lis Parsons 6 right, 10-11, 41, 45, 47, 52, 59, 63, 65, 71, 73, 75, 89, 91, 93, 95, 105, 115, 129, 139, 157, 163, 165, 191, 207; William Reavell 8 right, 9, 51, 67, 77, 81, 83, 99, 109, 159, 167, 199, 205, 211, 217, 219, 229, 231, 233; Craig Robertson 187; William Shaw 15, 19, 23, 29, 35, 39, 57, 107, 121, 123, 125, 133, 135, 137, 141, 143, 145, 147, 149, 155, 173, 175, 177, 179, 181, 185; Ian Wallace 102-103, 150-151.